2/23/08
Shirley
Thoughts create!

[signature: Jim]

EVERYDAY *Lessons*

Dear Shirley,
Enjoy the wonderful
journey !

Blessings
Catherine
2-23-08

EVERYDAY
Lessons

Understanding the Events,
Interactions, and Attitudes
That Make Up Your Life

• John F. Dull, M.A. • Margaret Ann Hollies • Catherine Poole, M.F.A. • James H. Schrenker, M.D.

integrated concepts publishing

Library of Congress Cataloging-in-Publication Data

Dull, John F., **Hollies**, Margaret Ann,
Poole, Catherine S., **Schrenker**, James H.

Everyday lessons: understanding the events, interactions,
and attitudes that make up your life/illustrated by
David W. Poole, Catherine S. Poole, M. Scott Mann

ISBN: 0-9759245-7-5 (Paperback)

1. Self-actualization (Psychology) 2. Mind and Body 3. Spirituality
4. New Age

I. Dull, John F. II. Title

PCN: 2004109485

An Integrated Concepts Publishing Premier Edition © 2004
Text Copyright © 2004
Cover Illustration Copyright © 2000 Anthony Droege

Printed in the United States of America

Integrated Concepts Publishing, LLC
P.O. Box 96
Middletown, IN 47356

A division of:
Integrated Concepts, LLC
Bluff City, TN 37618

Cover / Book Design:
M. Scott Mann, Tangent Design Group, Inc., Chicago, IL

Cover Illustration:
Anthony Droege, South Bend, IN

CONTENTS

Introduction: The Practice of Life Lessons

Chapter One: Free Will

CONTENTS

CONTENTS

CONTENTS

Chapter Seven: Hope

Chapter Eight: Spirit Guides

Chapter Nine: Crystals

Chapter Ten: Chakra Meditations

Conclusion

AUTHORS

John Dull, M.A.

Margaret Ann Hollies

Catherine Poole, M.F.A.

James H. Schrenker, M.D.

John Dull, M.A. has been actively involved in hypnotherapy for more than thirty years. He practiced hypnotherapy in Anderson, Indiana, following a long career as an educator and school administrator. He has lectured on hypnotherapy to members of the American Lung Association, various dental schools, and other organizations. John is a popular speaker for professional, educational, and civic groups.

Margaret Ann Hollies was the former general manager of a metaphysical resource center. She has studied religion and metaphysics for more than forty-five years. She has studied numerology and Gnothology with Eileen Connolly and mastered tarot with Thomas Green. She has organized and assisted with workshops featuring John Dull and other area talents for many years.

Catherine Poole, M.F.A. has a masters degree in graphic design from Cranbrook Academy of Art with a specialization in human response to color. She taught color theory and design at the University of Notre Dame for nine years and at Indiana University for five years. Catherine was a visiting professor in the philosophy department of Warsaw University in Warsaw, Poland. She has consulted with clients, including Reebok and Newell-Rubbermaid, concerning the subliminal use of color in advertising. She speaks and provides workshops on our spiritual relationship with color.

James H. Schrenker, M.D. is a practicing family physician in Bristol, Tennessee, and a graduate of Indiana University School of Medicine. He respects and uses his education and experience in conventional medicine while embracing metaphysical knowledge to provide the best possible care for his patients. With compassion and caring he fills a unique niche by educating and comforting souls as they prepare to make the transition to the other side. Dr. Schrenker speaks on a wide range of subjects throughout the United States.

DEDICATIONS

JOHN

I dedicate this book to my children and grandchildren.
I would also like to dedicate this book to the pioneers in regression
therapy who have paved the way: Leo Bolduc, Dr. Edith Fiore,
Dr. Bruce Goldberg, Lynn Sparrow, Dick Sutphen, Dr. Brian L. Weiss,
and others too numerous to mention.

MARGARET

I would like to dedicate this book to my children—
Hank, John, Sally, Catherine, and Jim—from whom I have
learned many lessons and hope I have taught a few.

CATHERINE

Hey, Dave, I love you. Thank you for your belief in our purpose,
your support, and input. Thank you to my children—Samuel, Sarah,
and Connor. Mom and Marge Aiman, your "kitchen table talks"
sculpted my beliefs; thanks for letting me stay and listen.

JAMES

To Erin and Allie, the brightest parts of my life.
Remember to ALWAYS follow your highest path.

This book is about identifying and understanding your life lessons. Just as a teacher sets her course for the school year with a lesson plan, we incarnate with our own "lesson plan." Accompanied with a set of goals and objectives, we, as our own teachers, arrive with lessons to learn and lessons to teach. The practice described here brings those lessons to your conscious and logical mind by asking you to simply *think about it*. It begins with one day, one Universal Truth, and your understanding that all events, interactions, and attitudes are lessons that make up a life—your life.

We bless and thank our spirit guides who illuminated our thoughts and brought us together in this process: Armulaen, Altazaar, Dr. Zest, Merta, and Roughan.

Also, a special thanks to Wendy Torrence for her valuable insight and suggestions. We appreciate your time and support.

INTRODUCTION

You have never heard this story before.

The seven Universal Truths shared in these pages were born from a lifetime of beliefs and practices. Their intimate partnership with color, weekdays, numbers, tone, and the chakras is so natural that you will find yourself repeatedly asking, "Why have I never heard this before?"

The Universal Truths have always existed, and now they are taught in a way so that you can easily garner the valuable knowledge they have to give. Understanding each truth will allow you to better cope with the events, relationships, and attitudes that make up your individual life in the form of Everyday Lessons.

The Practice

This book provides you with a practice for uncovering your life lessons by becoming aware of the seven Universal Truths of free will, karma, purity, love, truth, faith, and hope. Using this book as your companion, you will become conscious of one of these Universal Truths with the help of seven tools: a weekday, a color, a number, a musical note, a prayer, an affirmation, and a chakra meditation.

The Universal Truths

The Universal Truths of free will, karma, purity, love, truth, faith, and hope have been presented in order to provide guidance on our life journey. Spirit is the term used in this book to refer to the energy that each of us can access to gain wisdom and understanding in all our life planes. Whatever your beliefs, most people hold that a higher power exists. In this book we refer to this higher power as Spirit. While you are incarnated on this earth plane, these truths and the vibratory patterns representing them create a unique bridge to Spirit. Universal Truths make you more aware of your intuitive powers and metaphysical gifts. These gifts, often referred to as the sixth sense, are not the sole property of psychics or the clairvoyant. These intuitive powers are in all of us, and we must simply tune in to access them. This book teaches you how to use your intuition by creating relationships between your environment (physical and metaphysical) and yourself.

Universal Truths are not specific to any religion or spiritual agenda. They are part of the great design we call life. Although some may not understand or choose to live in accordance with the Universal Truths, everyone has access to them. They have been presented repeatedly throughout time under different names and in different religions and belief systems. They represent the universal characteristics of the collective consciousness: the Divine, Allah, Buddha, God, and every other manifestation of Spirit. The ultimate goal is the same for all—to practice unconditional love.

Life Lessons

By carrying out the practice described in this book, you will process and understand each Universal Truth from within your own life and not from someone else's experience. Your guardian angels and spirit guides are with you whether or not you have become aware of their presence. They will help you create awareness of the truths as you pass through your day. You will become aware of the little things, considering events, colors, and any vibration that may prompt you to think about a particular truth.

As you become aware of the manifestations of Universal Truths in everyday life, you will begin to look at situations and relationships from a different standpoint and view them as lessons. It is not a disaster. *It is a lesson.* It is not just true love. *It is a lesson.* It is not punishment or hardship. *It is a lesson.* That person is not stubborn or stupid. *Like me, he or she has lessons to give and to receive.*

No matter what is occurring in your life—good or bad, positive or negative—the important and vital element of your existence is life lessons. The practice described in this book will encourage you to constantly ask, "What can I learn from this?" and just as important, "What can I teach in this situation?" We are always learning unconditional love.

Each chapter provides tools that will help you identify and evaluate lessons learned and taught. Those lessons are about understanding the Universal Truths. When we understand the Universal Truths, we seek them out as qualities in others and ourselves.

Chapters of this book contain hypnotic regressions to current and previous incarnations. These sessions illustrate how clients have recognized, evaluated, and processed life lessons in their many forms. These can serve as examples for you in your daily practice of invoking life lessons that point toward the Universal Truths.

You have only two objectives in life.
They are teaching and learning.

The truth is simple—so simple it can be disappointing! We search for profound meaning and often convince ourselves it is difficult if not impossible to attain. In fact, it is right before us every day in the form of life lessons.

Recognize the Universal Truths of free will, karma, purity, love, truth, faith, and hope. Process them. Above all, respect their intent. Embrace their essence, and your life will flow forward. Resistance will only occur to keep life challenging, interesting, and evolving.

This relationship between the Universal Truths and their vibratory triggers will always foster a harmonic relationship between you and your environment.

Vibrations

The term *vibration* as used in this book is synonymous with energy. All matter contains life energy that is emitted in a specific pattern or a vibration. We can raise our vibration and energy toward the level of Spirit. Likewise, we can adjust our vibrations to match those humans that are on a different spiritual plane.

Everything from rocks to humans to air vibrates. Each Universal Truth carries a particular vibration. That vibration matches the vibration of a particular day of the week, a color, a number, and a musical tone. The day, color, number, and tone are *vibratory triggers* and will cue you to draw your attention to that particular Universal Truth.

The number seven sets forth a deeply significant pattern. There are seven Universal Truths, seven days of the week, seven colors in the prismatic spectrum, and seven musical whole notes in the scale. There are also seven major energy (chakra) points on the human body. This relationship between the Universal Truths and their vibratory triggers will always foster a harmonic relationship between you and your environment.

With this book as your companion, you can embrace and practice each Universal Truth, allowing your path to be lit and the vibratory patterns emanating from the world around you to be elevated.

How to Use This Book

Each chapter corresponds to a day of the week. The Universal Truth for that day of the week will be your companion. (For example, on Monday you will use the chapter "Monday: Free Will"). The day of the week, prayer, color, tone, number, and chakra meditation are reinforcements or reminders to help you invoke the Universal Truths as part of your daily routine.

Day of the Week

Assigning characteristics to certain days of the week is not a new practice. Monday is the first day of the workweek for many. For others, it may be library day or swimming day. Similarly, following the practice described in this book will help you identify each day with a Universal Truth. You are provided with a specific affirmation, a special prayer, and a meditation. You are invited to seek the vibratory triggers of color, tone, and number corresponding to that truth.

Each day begins with an affirmation. For example:

*Today I choose to be aware of choices I make
and how they affect others and me.*

The text describes a practice you can repeat every week on that day. Each Monday you will encounter different people, environments, experiences, and life lessons. These will present you with opportunities to embrace the Universal Truth of free will on Monday, karma on Tuesday, and so on.

Carrying out the practices described in this book will allow you to become less dependent on deliberate thought or action. When Monday comes, you will casually remember that it is a day of reflecting on choices, intent, and free will. You will begin to understand and process each of the seven Universal Truths on every day of the week, especially in situations in which you most need to call upon the truths. Eventually Monday will simply be a vibratory trigger that prompts you to think about the role of free will in your life. This will begin to occur not just on Mondays, but every day. We offer this practice so that you may understand and process the importance of the Universal Truths in a simple, easy way.

Focusing on a particular Universal Truth on a given day enables you to notice life lessons that otherwise would have passed you by. For example, while catalogue shopping for a perfect gift for Aunt Millie, you notice items fitting her personality. While looking through the same catalogue for your brother, you see an entirely different line of products. Likewise, if you spend your Monday dwelling on stress in your life, you will notice your accumulating obligations. If you make a conscious effort to look for free will in all of its manifestations, you will be aware of the power of your own freedom of choice.

Prayer

It has been said the difference between affirmation, prayer, and meditation is an affirmation is when we talk to self, a prayer is when we talk to Spirit, and meditation is when Spirit talks to us. Each day begins with a prayer in which we ask Spirit to help us invoke and pay attention to the Universal Truth of the day. With this prayer you cast the line, which will allow you to reel in the life lessons the day presents.

Recite the prayer. If you like, place a copy in a prominent yet personal place for you to glance at and recite as the day continues. Each prayer opens you to be more receptive in every situation you encounter that day and to every vibration transmitted in accordance with the given Universal Truth.

Color

Throughout the ages we have been exposed to color through environmental surroundings, art, clothing, and much more. The earliest written records of color belong to the Greeks (early fifth century B.C.). Aristotle believed in a seven-color scale because of color's relationship to music. Society still depends on the role of color as established thousands of years ago. These attitudes have subconsciously intertwined with our cultural roots. For example, school colors are derived from the banners displayed prominently during the Crusades. Our culture depends on these heraldic traditions, evident in wedding colors, prom colors, corporate colors, and colors utilized by other institutions as a specific portion of their identity.

Males and females see color differently. An explanation for this can be seen with the traditional hunter/gatherer theories. Rods and cones are the two basic types of photoreceptors existing in the retina. Rods have the visual pigment rhodopsin, which is sensitive to shorter wavelengths of light, i.e. blue/green. These are used for vision under low light conditions. Traditionally men became adept as hunters, turning their heads from side to side, hunting in the dim forests and at dusk, utilizing the rods in their retinas. The colors of blue and green are generally described as masculine colors, perhaps deriving from this association.

Females utilized the cones. Cones contain opsins as their visual pigments. Cones are sensitive to longer wavelengths of light, particularly reds, medium wavelengths of greens, and sometimes the shorter blue wavelengths. Females are associated with the gatherer characteristics because of their ability to see the colorful berries and nuts in the forest. These warmer female colors (pink for girls, blue for boys) find their origin from this association.

Color influences what we read, buy, eat, and feel. Despite being inherent in our lives, color is often taken for granted and not given proper respect. This book helps you cultivate a profound understanding of color and its connection to life lessons.

The visible aspect of the electromagnetic spectrum offers color. Color is on one end of the spectrum, and tone is on the other. Color can be thought of as visual tone. Music and color share much of the same vocabulary.

Color is transmitted using both physical materials and light. The study of color vibration through solid materials is known as reflective theory because it explores the reflection of color off a surface. When you see a red shirt, you are seeing the color red being reflected, not absorbed, by the surface of the shirt.

Because of technological advances we are constantly receiving color in its essential form of light, without reliance upon reflection. Color vibrations are transmitted into us from television, movie screens, and computer monitors. The vibrations of color, whether reflected off solid material or transmitted into you through light, affect you in some way, depending on the color, the amount of color, and environmental conditions. These effects are described in this book.

Each day of the week you will be introduced to the color vibrating to that day's Universal Truth. This book will offer you help in noticing color and its effects upon you and the world around you. It will help you draw the connection between the color as you experience it throughout the day and the Universal Truth to which you are seeking to become attuned.

Crystals are a particularly powerful means of bringing the color vibrations of the respective Universal Truth into your day. To learn more about using crystals in this way, see Chapter 9.

Tone

Tone can also be referred to as sound. Like color, tone can contribute to our well-being, healing, and invocation of the Universal Truths. Tone has an important place in everyday life. It is included in the sounds of nature, music, single musical keynotes, chants, speech, and more. The sound of the Universe is *"ohm."* It is the vocal sound for the crown chakra. It is translated as "I am" in many cultures. This sound acts as a purifier, compass, or reset button. By listening to the sounds of nature, prayers, or chakra meditations, either firsthand or on a recording, you can heighten your senses, alter your consciousness, and achieve a meditative state.

Regardless of the tone, every person is affected the same. Tone is energy in its most basic presentation. It has both amplitude and frequency. When the specific amplitude and frequency of a tone penetrate the body, it causes the atoms in the body to change their vibrations. This is known as sympathetic vibration. This change in the atoms can bring a body into balance. When a body is in balance, it is more susceptible to care/cure. The energy of tone carries the Universal Truths. For example, the vocal sound of a long "O" (as in "tone") and the musical keynote of D correspond to the Universal Truth of karma. By introducing yourself to this tone, with or without music, your body's vibrations are prepared to accept and understand the objectives of that truth.

This book provides you with the needed musical keynote and suggests ways to bring it into your life. By activating and opening our chakras, tone acts as an important vehicle for transferring energy between mind and matter and connects our physical being to the spiritual plane.

Numbers

The study of numbers dates back to the Greek philosopher and mathematician Pythagoras (born in 580 B.C.). It is because of his interest in the study of numbers that numerology, the science of numbers, has been around for over 2500 years. Pythagoras based his theory on the numbers from 1-9 and that man's evolution had nine levels. Numerology associates each number with a characteristic, and the vibrations are similar to the corresponding color.

Everything around you is identified through numerical listings: license plates, addresses, social security numbers, phone numbers, birthdays, even time. The list is endless. This section is to create awareness of numbers as a vibratory trigger. In order to figure out what numbers are surrounding you at a given time, simply reduce the group of numbers to one digit. For example, the date is 4-23-2004. This adds up to 15 (4+2+3+2+4=15), which is a 6 (1+5). Six vibrates to the Universal Truth of faith. You will be aware of life lessons involving concern for others, recognizing the positive qualities in others, and other 6 vibrations when that particular number is put in your path.

Chakra Meditation

Each Universal Truth is associated with one of the body's seven major chakras. The chakra meditations bring your focus to the respective chakra. The meditations will act as a guide through the process of infusing that chakra with the color of the day's Universal Truth and joining it with the energizing, purifying white light of Spirit. You are given instructions on how to incorporate a crystal into this practice.

Meditation, as well as prayer and affirmation, can be used at any time during your day. A meditation is presented to assist you in evaluating and acknowledging the lessons and encounters experienced throughout the day. Meditation is concentration and introspection. Unlike prayer, it is not a request for assistance. Meditation opens your subconscious mind, creating an intimate relationship with your physical, mental, and spiritual self. The meditations described in this book heighten your sensitivity to spiritual insights by quieting your body and mind so that your spirit may listen. Meditation is even more beneficial than a power nap during the course of a workday.

There are many books on meditation techniques. Meditation is a personal process, and each person is encouraged to develop a style effective for them. There is no wrong way to meditate because it is the intent behind the meditation that establishes success.

Chakra Diagram

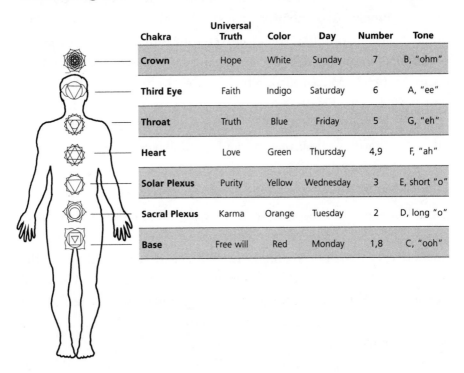

Chakra	Universal Truth	Color	Day	Number	Tone
Crown	Hope	White	Sunday	7	B, "ohm"
Third Eye	Faith	Indigo	Saturday	6	A, "ee"
Throat	Truth	Blue	Friday	5	G, "eh"
Heart	Love	Green	Thursday	4,9	F, "ah"
Solar Plexus	Purity	Yellow	Wednesday	3	E, short "o"
Sacral Plexus	Karma	Orange	Tuesday	2	D, long "o"
Base	Free will	Red	Monday	1,8	C, "ooh"

CHAPTER ONE

monday

Universal Truth: *Free Will*

Chakra: *Base* ~ Color: *Red* ~ Numbers: *1, 8*

Musical Keynote: *Middle C*

Vocal Sound: *"Ooh"*

Affirmation: *I am aware of my choices.*

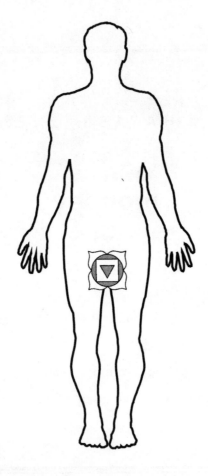

Chakra: *Base*

Eve chose to bite into the apple, thus starting
the "fall of mankind." Not only was this the
beginning of free will, but
it was also the beginning of all karmic processes.

Free will is the first Universal Truth. Free will is what makes us human. The first chakra, or energy point in the body, is known as the root chakra and vibrates in accordance with the color red and with free will. It is this chakra that roots us to the earth. The numbers 1 and 8 both vibrate to the Universal Truth of free will.

Monday is the first workday of the week for many. It is a day to begin to change the way you perceive your life and the situations around you. Using the practices described below, you will come to notice and exercise ways in which you can use your power to make choices that positively affect you and others throughout the day. You will see opportunities to direct yourself toward your highest path through all decisions, from quitting a job to eating a greasy hamburger.

Guidance is always there.
Choosing to listen is up to us.

As you look for and exercise opportunities to make good choices, you can and will change your life. You will appreciate all events and encounters as lessons, not hardships, painful experiences, or troublesome relationships. As time goes by, you will begin to reflect more on your life. You will begin to see the beauty in each and every moment. You will begin to rejoice in the lessons you are learning.

Begin with the simple realization that all choices you make impact your life and the lives of others. Most of all, give thanks to God for granting you free will.

Red: The Color of Free Will

Red is associated with free will. *Adam,* according to Judeo-Christian tradition, is the name of the first man. *Adam* means red and earth. The apple associated with Adam and Eve is a representation of the color red. *Adam* can also be considered in the context of the *atom,* referring to a source of energy that makes up matter.

As shown in the chakra meditation (Chapter 10) on free will, red activates and vibrates with the first chakra, which is the root chakra and our energy base. This chakra deals with all human emotions. Emotions are the drive for free will. Red, the root chakra, and free will are where it all begins.

Red is the color of heat and friction. It is a color of quickness, swift change, and fast beginnings. It is the color of fire. We associate fire with heat and destruction, yet fire is needed sometimes to seed the forest or the farmland and to begin anew.

Red is perceived more negatively than any other color in our society. It symbolizes raw human emotions that are intense, wide-ranging, and unpredictable. It can also be associated with fear and control. Yet, when choices abound, we must invoke our free will in order to make the right decision. Red is anger and pain, but it is also energy and change. Red stimulates the release of adrenaline into the blood stream. Red gives us the impetus to begin new experiences. It is a vital vibratory force that can aid us in exercising our free will.

In color therapy, red can loosen muscles and relieve joint aches. Red is helpful in reconditioning paralyzed muscles and beneficial in an environment utilizing physical therapy. It helps with circulation. The warm, stimulating qualities can be beneficial to persons who catch chills and colds easily. Warm red (red pushing to orange) in an office environment not only increases productivity, but also cuts down on heating bills. Using the color red in your personal environment will bring about awareness of choices and the consequences of those choices.

Throughout your day:

- Wear red, seen or unseen. Begin to associate the color red, wherever it may be, with free will.

- Red demands a choice of action. Approach your tasks with the best of intentions.

- Drink from a red glass or cup.
- Notice red in your environment, in traffic, sale signs, and important information. Where is red most prominently displayed? Notice that little else is needed to get your attention!
- Get a massage!
- Discuss freewill associations with others.

1, 8: The Numbers of Free Will

Individuality vibrates to the number 1. Vibrating to the Universal Truth of free will, the numerological characteristics of the number 1 are:

- Courage
- Originality
- Opinionated
- Determination
- Independence
- Energetic

The power of leadership vibrates to the number 8. Vibrating to the Universal Truth of free will, the numerological characteristics of the number 8 are:

- Supervisory
- Good Judgment
- Strength
- Efficiency
- Organization
- Materialism

Middle C: The Musical Keynote of Free Will

The musical keynote of C is the correct auditory vibration for the truth of free will. If the key of C were visible, it would vibrate to the color red. It has the vocal sound of "ooh."

Understanding the Universal Truth of Free Will

Free will is the willingness to be in control of your actions and make choices. It is your choices that direct you through this life of learning. The opportunities you choose to take advantage of, as well as ignore, shape your soul.

If we have no choice, there is no lesson.
If we can learn the lesson, there is no wrong choice.

Free Will Is the Greatest Gift

Even though God could make us follow His every command and every wish, Spirit has given us the ability to decide for ourselves between right and wrong. In the Judeo-Christian tradition, Eve exercised free will by tasting the apple and offering it to Adam. Adam exercised free will by eating it. They asked, "What if?" Then they asked, "Why not?" God gave them free will, and they had a choice to obey or disobey God. This led to the fall of mankind and a state in which humans determine their own actions and live with and learn from the consequences.

This story is just one traditional way of describing how Spirit gave us free will and what we are expected to do with it. Free will is a gift. Our lives have more meaning when we are aware of our decision to choose the right path, the highest path. If we have no

---

choice, there is no lesson. If we can learn the lesson, there is no wrong choice. Coupled with intent, free will is a very important aspect of our development.

The past cannot be changed. The future is yet
in your power. —*Hugh White*

Pure Intent Is More Important Than Good Consequences

Pause for a moment to reflect on a goal you have pursued. It may relate to your career, education, family, or finances. The goal can be called intent because it represents what you intended to do. Intent is a human phenomenon not needed by Spirit. Spirit guides have attained a higher vibratory level than man and do not need intent. God resides at the highest vibratory level. Intent is meaningful to humans because it allows us to learn, grow, and establish goals.

Intent is driven by emotion. Think again about your goal. What emotions motivated you to pursue it? Did the degree or strength of your emotions have a strong bearing on the outcome of your actions? Think not just in terms of outcomes, but also of the lessons you learned. Most likely you'll find that actions motivated by pure intent resulted in important lessons in your life. Strong feelings of love, joy, resentment, or greed are examples of pure intent.

Intent is a fundamental aspect of life.
It is the intent behind the situation that gives
the situation its ultimate meaning.

The lesson is learned when the intent is pure. The lesson is in how you approach a situation and what you learn from it, regardless of the outcome. The lesson may not be the achievement of a particular goal, but the joy of the journey. When you become conscious of a choice you are making, ask yourself, "What emotion or intent is behind this choice? What can be changed in the world with this attitude?" Whether your actions are grand or seemingly insignificant, you are ultimately responsible for them. If your intent is pure, good things will follow. Things happen for a reason; things always work out for the best.

Akashic Records: Your Book of Life

The Akashic Record is your Book of Life. Your Akashic Records track your lessons and your karmic paths; think of this as cosmic record keeping. If you have the intent to do harm, yet no harm is done, the action is still considered negative. It results in a negative emotional imprint being recorded in your Akashic Record. Likewise, if you have good intentions, but a negative outcome results, that action is considered positive. The example below illustrates this difference.

> *Out of a desire for safety, well-being, and freedom for the members of his village, a local leader in Cuba leaves for Florida in a small boat, taking thirty-five people with him. On the way, the boat sinks under huge waves, and twenty-one people die.*
>
> *How is this recorded in his Akashic Record? Because his intent was pure, the action is considered positive, although it is viewed in our world as disastrous.*
>
> *The twenty-one people who died exercised their free will in making the choice to escape to freedom. Even though he was ultimately responsible for their deaths, the leader's intent was pure; he genuinely tried to help the others.*

We can take comfort in knowing our goals are still achievable, no matter what choices we make. The path to a goal may be long and hard or delightful and pleasant. Life is not about achieving a goal as much as it is about learning the lessons of the journey. The more opportunities we have to learn, the more fulfilling our path is.

A decision is only wrong if you choose not to learn the lessons it presents. In fact, the longer you ignore those lessons, the longer you may be stuck in a painful or unpleasant situation.

There will be detours on your path. You will go in unforeseen directions. Remember, the path less traveled is often the one that holds more beauty and growth. Spirit will always present you with choices to put you once again on a more direct path. Taking advantage of those opportunities will be a matter of exercising your free will.

> *After finding my partner, spending ten good years with her and having two wonderful daughters together, I found myself disconnected from Spirit and feeling alone. I began a remarkable year of change, which finds me single again and deeply connected with my children. My reconnection with Spirit is electric. My path is much clearer, more exciting, and much more meaningful. In short, I learned much in ten years. I did not make a wrong choice or waste any time. Spirit has been able to see the whole picture and to help accelerate my healing. It is comforting to know there are no "wrong choices," just different paths to take. Guidance is always there. Choosing to listen is up to us. —Dr. Schrenker*

With Free Will Comes Responsibility

Too often we think of free will as something that affects only the person who exercises it. Every decision we make affects and is affected by all beings and the entire vibratory pattern of the earth plane. One decision can change the paths of thousands of souls.

While the individual exercises free will, karma intertwines the path of that individual with the paths of multiple beings throughout multiple lifetimes. Although the Universal Truth of karma is associated with Tuesday and will be discussed at length in the following chapter, it is intimately connected to free will and so will be discussed here.

Karma is often described as similar to the ripple effect of the stone tossed into the pond. By exercising free will, by making decisions and taking action, we affect others' life paths. Our choices and actions send ripples through the lives of others both present and past. When a soul is given the opportunity to learn a lesson in one lifetime and does not take that opportunity, he or she will face the same lesson in other lifetimes until it is learned. Sometimes we encounter people whose actions provide or deny us the opportunity to learn the lessons we need to learn. Always remember, another's lesson may depend on our actions. By making a conscious freewill decision, we can end or start karmic relationships.

Free will allows you to take advantage of
opportunities that fulfill karmic obligations.

In the course of exercising our own free will, we must always protect that of others. One of the greatest wrongs that can be committed is to impinge upon another's free will. Sadly, we see this behavior often in our world through the actions of dictators, murderers, rapists, and anyone who abuses humans, nature, or animals. By infringing on others' free will, we create karma that needs to be worked out in the future. By using free will, you choose whose life you will touch and change. At some level the other soul has to consent to be involved. Souls have complex relationships that exist outside of the earth plane. The people whom you touch have consented to be with you and work with you during this life, particularly the difficult souls that challenge you and your beliefs!

Freewill Actions Can Lead Us to Karmic Clarity

Occasionally by exercising our free will, we encounter and resolve a karmic lesson or a problem left over from a past life. We may have a sudden feeling like a light bulb has been turned on. Spirit refers to this moment as karmic clarity. In this moment we experience enlightenment.

Enlightenment occurs when we are aware of the lessons offered by our immediate circumstances. In future lives you will encounter circumstances similar to those that led to your moments of karmic clarity in this life. You'll move through these moments with more ease. Moments of karmic clarity allow us the comfort of knowing we have exercised our free will to its fullest potential. Life offers us countless opportunities to fulfill karmic obligations. Free will allows us to take advantage of these opportunities.

Hardship Is Not Necessary

Though we often associate lessons with hardship, they need not be painful. We choose how we will learn our lessons by using our free will. Many times we choose the path of hardship. We feel if the lesson is to be learned, then we should struggle and suffer. However, any lesson can be learned just as fully through abundance, joy, love, and gratitude. We are offered these qualities each and every day. They are just as effective as any form of hardship in allowing us to learn lessons, but we must be aware of the potential for learning lessons through such subtle forms.

Take, for example, the man who experienced abundance in a past life. He did not exercise his free will to share that abundance with others. He did not learn the lessons associated with appreciating abundance, nor could he help others learn those lessons. Instead, he chose to pass into the next life and learn the lessons of abundance there. When choosing his next incarnation he felt that hardship would accelerate his learning. He chose to incarnate as an impoverished child starving in Africa. It is not simply his situation in this life that affects him, but his circumstances and the choices he made in a previous life. These choices have helped his soul plan the lesson he is learning. There are many avenues for learning the same lesson, just as there are countless ways in which we can affect karma through free will.

Case Study in Free Will

Media carried the story of a 17-year-old girl who needed to have a multiple organ transplant in order to live. She received the organs, but they were of the wrong blood type. Due to the mistake, she only had 48 hours to live after the transplant. With only 24 hours left, the family of a child whose body was being kept alive made the difficult decision to turn off the machines and donate their child's organs. Being of the correct blood type, the organs were implanted, and the girl was given a new chance at life. Unfortunately, she soon passed away.

How can this be free will? The parents of both donors exercised free will in an extremely difficult situation. The intent was pure, but in the end the young girl's contract called for her to go. All souls involved, including the doctors, nurses, and others, learned valuable lessons.

Exercising free will can be looked at in a much simpler arena. You choose to be aware of the implications involved through positive reactions versus negative overreactions. Rather than becoming worked up or aggravated at a railroad crossing, you choose to understand the freight train does not care. It is not affected by your inability to get to work or home on time.

Perhaps you, for the first time, witness the building of road rage within yourself. Contributed by the hypnotic effect of the surrounding red taillights, you choose to understand traffic does not care. Instead of allowing the red to aggravate and stimulate in a negative manner, allow your conscious mind to be aware of your freewill choices and the choices of others.

What could be seemingly harmless gestures used to express frustrations may contribute or cause a series of chain events that affect many individuals. You gesture to someone, and he/she arrives home in a foul mood and takes that out on a spouse or a child, who in turn takes his/her frustration out on others. It is a cycle that never ends, so choose to spin it in a positive direction!

Periodically throughout the day when you notice red, think to yourself, "Red represents free will, and I need to be aware that the choices I make can affect everyone." Choose with pure intent.

Affirmation of Free Will

Today I choose to be aware of choices I make and how they affect others and myself.

Prayer for Free Will

Spirit, it is with a humble heart that I ask for the inner knowledge to make the right choices in my life. I am striving to understand the loving nature of free will and ask You to manifest wisdom in my heart so that I may gain knowledge in my soul. It is through free will that I begin to consider and honor the importance of other souls in my life's path. I ask You to help me use this knowledge to fulfill your highest and most loving intentions. May I attain the divine, holy state of being that You intend for me, I pray. Amen.

CHAPTER TWO

tuesday

Universal Truth: *Karma*

Chakra: *Sacral Plexus* ~ Color: *Orange* ~ Number: *2*

Musical Keynote: *D*

Vocal Sound: *Long "O" as in "tone"*

Affirmation: *I am aware of my intentions.*

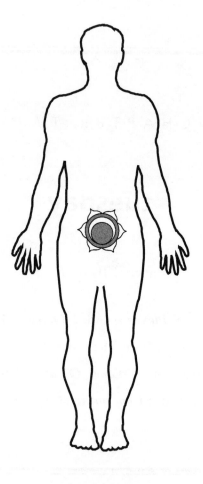

Chakra: *Sacral Plexus*

It is a privilege to be here. Every soul that has chosen to be here has the capacity to understand its purpose.

Karma is the second Universal Truth. The color orange is a vibratory trigger for karma. The second chakra, or energy point in the body, is known as the sacral chakra. The number 2 vibrates to the Universal Truth of karma.

Karma is a Sanskrit word meaning action. Karma, simply put, is a lesson plan. Karma is the overall package of lessons, goals, and objectives. Karmic lessons involve action, reaction, and interaction.

There is a difference in the definition of goals and objectives. Many individuals use these words interchangeably, but from a teaching standpoint they are very different. Examine objectives and goals carefully. Goals are an established, finite set of criteria. Objectives are the side benefits. For example, while learning patience you may achieve the objective of learning compassion for another's situation.

Karma is all events, major or minor, that help form your life. Do not be misdirected into thinking an event must be major in order to be life changing. A perfectly timed observation by one human to another can be life altering. One statement or inference made by someone you respect can stay with you for an entire lifetime. Are you a workaholic? Was this manifested from a casual remark in your childhood about being lazy?

All events—whether seemingly tragic, heinous, joyous, or profound—are the result of complicated and interwoven relationships with the wild card of free will thrown in. Free will, as stated in the previous chapter, works both ways. The defining factor in terms of karmic ramifications is intent. Even with intent defined and understood, the role of forgiveness is by far the most influential aspect of karma. These events that make up a life should be examined for what they are—lessons to fulfill your karmic goals.

Orange: The Color of Karma

The color associated with karma is orange. Orange is the color defining creative action. It represents the ways in which humans interact with our environment. Orange is a color prompting creative obser-vation. It is a color that should prompt the question *Why?* "Why do I feel this way about this person? Why does this house feel creepy? Why do I love dogs? Why am I afraid of water?" Where red can be overpowering, orange holds a quiet strength that can move mountains.

In color therapy, orange is used to treat asthma, bronchitis, and other lung problems. Depression, grief, and profound loss are commonly treated with the color orange because it promotes a healthy attitude.

The color orange inspires a cheerful, logical, and most often intense observation to some of our most confusing situations. In the chakra meditation on karma, orange vibrates in accordance with the second chakra, the sacral chakra that governs the intestinal area. Orange resides at the intersection of red and yellow. Creativity abounds at this meeting point between new beginnings of the root chakra and the intellect, ego of the solar plexus chakra.

Orange can promote a healthy outlook on life. It provides us with the energy to creatively observe our environment and examine the creative karmic relationships that lie within. This generation experi-enced orange in the 1970s. There is a resurgence of orange as current culture is defined with an eerily corresponding set of circumstances. We are involved in a controversial war, divided loyalties regarding human rights, and a younger generation attempting to reestablish the focus on love and tolerance, not hate and bigotry.

Orange is environmental in the arena of clothes, small products, and limited interior fashion. All of these products are eventually disposable. Using the color orange in your personal environment should bring about awareness of the circumstances and the forces leading to various actions and the actions of others.

It is a color of independence. Orange is courage to accept and change what is necessary. Orange resides over the intestines, and it is no coincidence that it is represented by the term *gut instinct.*

Throughout your day:

- On Tuesday wear orange, seen or unseen.

- Begin your day drinking orange juice!

- Let orange take you out of the box. Examine the interactions you never think about. What actions, reactions, and interactions do you take for granted? Ask why and then be open to the answer.

- Think about your interactions with others. Examine relationships that need work or explanations. Write a name and the situation on a piece of orange paper. For example, "Why do I feel so warm and welcomed when I walk into a friend's house?" or "Why do I not trust this colleague even though she has always been so nice to me?"

- Before bringing orange specifically into your environment, observe where it is already displayed. Ask what could be understood about karmic relationships involving that environment.

- Put orange on your desk.

- Drink your beverage from an orange glass or cup.

- Charge your crystal with the power of orange. What situations keep repeating themselves? Are you always out of money? Are you constantly apologizing to certain people? Meditate with your crystal and ask those questions. What can you change by understanding your observations, goals, and objectives?

- Use the power of this crystal and the color orange to quit smoking, heal your lungs, and open your mind and body to fresh air.

2: The Number of Karma

The 2 vibration is the number for sharing. Vibrating to the Universal Truth of karma, the numerological characteristics of this number are:

- Cooperation
- Partnership
- Peace
- Tact
- Consideration

D: The Musical Keynote of Karma

The musical keynote of D is the correct auditory vibration for the truth of karma. If the key of D were visible, it would vibrate to the color of orange. The vocal equivalent to this is the long "O" sound as in the word "tone."

Understanding the Universal Truth of Karma

Karma is used primarily in connection with the Eastern religions of Buddhism and Hinduism. Recently it has been revived by New Agers and subsequently bastardized by popular society and the media.

You may be familiar with the following representations of karma:

- "What goes around comes around"
- Cause-and-effect
- Action-reaction
- "For whatsoever a man soweth, that shall he also reap" (Gal. 6:7)
- "Whoso sheddeth man's blood, by man shall his blood be shed" (Gen. 9:6)

In this book, the Universal Truth of karma is defined as the lessons we learn through interaction with ourself, others, the Earth, and the Universe.

How Understanding Karma Helps Us

Understanding the Universal Truth of karma helps us cope with life's challenges. By understanding karma you have less need to place judgment or become overwhelmed with emotion in a difficult situation. The situation was planned before this incarnation as a way for you and others to learn a particular lesson. Increasingly, you can look at the situation objectively and exercise your free will to advance spiritually. Rather than dwelling on past injustices, you bring about understanding, release, and then forgiveness.

The Universal Truth of karma gives reason to our suffering. Spirit, out of love, has given us more than one chance to correct our mistakes. Karma is always an opportunity for a lesson and should not be viewed as retribution or punishment. This is represented by an illustration from Christian tradition. Jesus and his disciples walk past a man who has been blind since birth. The disciples ask Jesus, "Master, who did sin, this man, or his parents, that he was born blind?" Jesus answers, "Neither hath this man sinned, nor his parents: but that the works of God should be made manifest in him" (John 9:1–3). For this question to have been asked of Christ indicates karma was a feasible possibility.

The advances we can make by understanding karma are demonstrated by many of the case studies of past-life regressions provided in this chapter. Hypnotherapist John Dull, one of the authors of this book, conducted the regressions. The names of those involved have been fictionalized.

Reincarnation

Karma links one soul to different bodies in different lifetimes. These lifetimes are also known as incarnations. Karma consists of the lessons you have learned in past and present incarnations, as well as those you have yet to learn. Karma is like a book in which all of your acts and thoughts are written. Each chapter contains a lifetime.

Each paragraph represents an event in that lifetime that led you to learn a particular life lesson. Each paragraph is specific to only one chapter. Once a lesson has been learned, it need not be re-learned in another lifetime.

When finished, the book, often referred to as your Akashic Record, is the same for all. Everyone needs to learn the same lessons. Some wish to start at chapter one; others, at chapter ten. When finished, the book is closed. You are then released from the wheel of karma. Your soul has learned its lessons and does not have to incarnate again, although it may choose to do so.

The Karmic Contract and Relationships

Between lifetimes as your soul prepares to return to earth, it meets with other souls and spirit guides, some with whom you have had relationships. You are karmically linked with these souls, and with them you will plan the lessons that are to be worked on in future lifetimes. There are some circumstances in which you teach and others in which you learn. It depends on how you look at the situation. You make agreements called karmic contracts.

As you encounter those with whom you have karmic links, you may feel an overwhelming familiarity, as if you had known them all your life. You may be inexplicably drawn to someone and feel a lasting sense of security from the encounter, but you may never see that person again. Karmic links involve lessons whether in the form of small events or major upheavals.

You have only two objectives in life.
You teach and you learn.

Those ready to reincarnate are brave and ambitious. They may choose to become involved with a person, group, or cause that provides great challenges and multiple lessons. In choosing to resolve karma they may choose to interact with nature or their environment rather than people. They may be challenged with a disability or a natural disaster. The following transcription of a past-life regression illustrates how our souls determine the content of our karmic contracts:

> *Peggy: I chose to come down as a teacher and teach many children. It seems like the early 1700s. I am a teacher in England, teaching all boys. I am a man, too. I don't think we educated girls much then.*
>
> *JD: What feelings do you have as that male teacher?*
>
> *Peggy: It is our duty to inspire these children to a good life. We have to do what we have to do. We have a rod and we pound 'em good. 'Spare the rod and spoil the child.' I am stern but I am not cruel. The name of the school is Bechal School for Boys.*
>
> *JD: How old are these boys?*
>
> *Peggy: Ages 9 and 10. It is a prep school.*
>
> *JD: Do they wear uniforms?*
>
> *Peggy: As best they can. Dark pants with a light shirt.*
>
> *JD: Do you have a strong sense of Empire? [pertaining to England]*
>
> *Peggy: Yes, we have to be very firm. We have to teach what we really don't believe ourselves—for the good of the country, you know. We have to teach that these are children of the people who own all this land, and they have minions working for them with no say. These boys have to be taught how to get the most out of people who farm their land. They are*

upper class; they will go out and own land and small villages on their land. They have to be responsible for the people under them.

JD: What is your name?

Peggy: Ephram.

JD: Last name?

Peggy: Hosier.

JD: Let's move ahead to an important event that may affect your life now.

Peggy: I have some students, three—they are teacher's pets. They get by with things that the others don't get by with. They can leave the room more often or not have to sit so straight. They are very nice young men. We are having some kind of holiday celebration; everyone is dancing. They are using the schoolroom as a meetinghouse. It is a celebration; someone is getting married or something. Everyone is very happy.

JD: Does Ephram ever marry?

Peggy: No.

JD: Does he have a superior that he likes or answers to?

Peggy: He is hired by the fathers of the boys to do the teaching. He is pretty much his own man.

JD: Step out into your higher self and know why Ephram's lifetime impacted you as Peggy in this lifetime.

Peggy: These three boys that I was partial to, I know them in this life as my son-in-law, his son (my grandson), and my other son-in-law. They weren't friends, but they were the ones I was partial to. I was just drawn to them.

JD: Have you been with them in a previous life, besides as Ephram and Peggy?

Peggy: Yes, I have been with them many times.

JD: Let's move on to moments before Ephram crosses over [dies].

Peggy: He is on his way to a meeting, his horse falls into a hole and throws him, and he breaks his neck. His spirit leaves.

JD: From your higher self, look back and draw some conclusions. First, how would you summarize Ephram Hosier?

Peggy: Basically a good man, loved to teach people. He thought a lot of that life, yet it was so solitary. A lot of his concentration went into training those young men. His life as a whole was lonely, but he enjoyed the people that he touched.

JD: What were you doing while you were on the other side, immediately following your death as Ephram Hosier?

Peggy: I was probably learning different things, but it was more observation, observing people. Learning how to be and how not to be, but very detached, without emotion.

Peggy's contract included a lesson on the ability to touch lives through quiet kindness and a sense of duty. She was initially regressed because she was curious about the relationships with individuals around her. She realized the circumstances were familiar and why she felt connected to their lives. Likewise, they hold a quiet respect for her.

Contract Moments

When you suddenly feel that the scene unfolding around you has happened before, this is called déjà vu, French for "already seen." You may seem to know what another person is going to say before it is said or know what you are about to see before you see it. Déjà vu sometimes occurs when a prophetic dream stored in the subconscious mind is stimulated by real experience. Some researchers believe déjà vu is a trick of the mind in which information is processed so quickly that it seems to have happened long before. Déjà vu often relates to memories of a past life.

Along your path you will have moments which give you the feeling that what is happening is supposed to happen. Perhaps you walk through a doorway and suddenly know the phone will ring, or you may have a dream played out shortly thereafter in reality. Spirit refers to these occurrences as contract moments. Contract moments are reassurance that you are on the proper path. Contract moments foster faith. Think of them as a pat on the back from your spirit guide.

> *While traveling in The Hague, Netherlands, Rebecca exited the tram and walked toward the neighborhood where she would be staying. Though she had never been there, everything seemed and smelled very familiar. She knew the location of the coffee shop, the chocolate shop, and many other merchants, not by sight, but by innate sense of guidance and smells. She was never homesick and felt comfortable.*
>
> *A year or so later she was regressed to help with weight loss. Rebecca also wanted to discover why she had become obsessed with the scent, not the taste, of chocolate and coffee. Another discovery during the regression was why she detested the chore of laundry. During the session she revealed that she was a young, blonde, blue-eyed Jewish girl living in The Hague. Her parents, in the hope her origins would not be discovered by the Germans, sent her out into the streets. Starving in an alley and searching for food, Rebecca was picked up by German soldiers. She was sent to a camp and immediately was put to work cleaning German officers' uniforms. An accident blinded her, but the compassion of the camp commandant allowed her to be released.*

Rebecca's visit to The Hague brought back the past life memories as they related to her current situation. Asked to examine these memories in the context of life lessons, Rebecca was able to understand the correlation between contract moments and past life experiences.

Karmic Debt

Karma always works toward balance. Think of it as a bank account which you add to or deduct from depending on your actions. The goal of your existence is to achieve a balance of zero by learning life's lessons.

As we live our lives, it is easy to forget the situations when we did not act with the best intentions. These events are hidden deep in the subconscious mind. Like it or not, the bill is due and will be paid in this incarnation or in a future one. Since we are solely responsible for absolutely everything that has ever happened to us, there is no one else to blame. Imagine a world in which people know they are responsible for all of their actions. If karma is not balanced in this lifetime, one has to come back repeatedly and experience similar lessons until things are made right. There would be less crime and ugliness in the world if this knowledge were widespread.

People often believe there is nothing they can do to change their karma. They believe it is predestined or fated, but this is not always the case. Karma is active. We create our own karma and are also the only ones who can change it. Wisdom and free will can change karma.

Karmic Remnants

A karmic remnant is an extraneous reverberation of a karmic lesson already learned in a previous lifetime. It seems out of place or anomalous amid the normal flow of our lives, but it need not have a great impact. A karmic remnant can consist of an idiosyncratic behavior or emotional baggage carried across other lifetimes into this one.

The behavior associated with a karmic remnant cannot be logically explained. It may consist of a compulsive disorder, phobia, or erratic behavior. On occasion, medical problems such as asthma or rashes can be traced to karmic remnants.

A karmic remnant can be carried across lifetimes attached to a certain sight, smell, sound, taste, or touch.

Matt had always hated the smell of lilacs. He would become nauseated with prolonged exposure.

His mother had taken him to doctors for allergy tests, which showed nothing to be wrong. As a young adult Matt often felt sad and depressed after smelling lilacs.

The condition seemed to worsen as he approached his twenty-third birthday. Seeking the help of a hypnotherapist, he was regressed to an incarnation chosen by his subconscious mind.

It was 1874. He was a clerk in a general store, age twenty-three. His wife was expecting their second child, and there were complications. The doctor was called when she began hemorrhaging.

The day was hot, and the house was open to catch any trace of wind. Outside the bedroom window was a lilac bush in bloom. The strong fragrance filled the bedroom as the doctor worked in vain to save the young woman and her baby. The young man watched helplessly in tears as he lost his beloved wife and son.

Matt's subconscious was asked to explain why he had brought this karmic remnant into this lifetime. He explained that he had never let go of his grieving and sadness. He had never remarried and was still grieving when he passed on at age sixty-one.

The therapist brought Matt back to the present and asked him to remain in the trance state. Matt volunteered his current concern; he and his wife had tried for many years but had been unable to conceive. The therapist asked Matt's subconscious what needed to be done to put the problem to rest. Matt answered, "To accept the fact the event was another time, another place, and let it go."

The therapist, addressing Matt's subconscious mind, said, "Work on putting this problem behind you and raise your right hand when this has been accomplished." Only two or three minutes passed before Matt raised his hand.

Matt recovered and, relieved of the stress and anxiety, he soon became a father.

The senses are not the only potential triggers of karmic remnants. Hypnosis, meditation, yoga, trances, scrying (mirror or crystal gazing), bodywork, and rhythmic activities can bring a karmic remnant to the surface.

Not all karmic remnants are negative. A karmic remnant may show up as a special talent or skill. Mozart, playing music and composing at age five, may have been continuing a talent from a previous life. It may manifest in knowledge of a subject you have never studied or an inexplicably strong emotional connection to a person or activity. Perhaps a young football player donning his gear before a big game receives flashes of memory of girding for a jousting tournament in Old England or preparing for battle as a Roman legionnaire. He may disregard these as memories of a movie he has seen, but it is often more significant.

Unexplained talents, phobias, or habits may have an impact on an individual's life and karmic path. Your reactions to these karmic remnants may fulfill or block your current karmic contract. Understanding the behavior and moving forward (picking up where one left off, so to speak) is the lesson to be learned. Focusing on these remnants should be examined for intent. Positive and healthy views can only enhance one's life journey.

The following hypnotic past-life regression shows how a karmic remnant can be triggered by something as seemingly insignificant as putting on panty hose or being around water. The woman seeking the regression, Johanna, sought help overcoming a fear of being on a boat or near a large body of water. She also had a strong aversion to anything that constrained her lower legs. She slept with her ankles uncovered and would experience stress when putting on her slacks or panty hose. She had regressed to a life as a sailor. He had lost fingers working on the whaling ship *Charles & Henry*. Although she had never been to the coast, she described its sounds and smells. Her voice had taken on the accent of an old sailor.

> *Joanna: 'Whale Ho! Ahead to starboard, the Captain wants one more to 'cap off the take.'*
>
> *The boats are lowered and manned. There is furious rowing toward the whales. There seems to be a whole pod of whales. The harpooner stands ready. As we get closer to the whales, the harpooner casts. There is a stick; the line begins to play out furiously. When the line is all out, it will be drawn. The whale will tow the boat, and that will wear the whale out. Then the men can take it. My job is to keep water on the peg [the post around which the line is played out].*
>
> *As the line plays out, I somehow gets [sic] the line caught up around me legs and ankles. In an instant, I am jerked out of the boat, off the side, and down into the sea.*
>
> *It all happened so fast yet in slow motion. I had time enough to think, 'Damn, I have done this job so many times, so often. Why did I get careless now, on this, my last run on my way home?' I had to fight to reach down to get the knife out of my belt to cut the rope off from around my legs.*

But the speed of the whale and the way in which it's dragging me down makes [sic] it impossible. The pain is shooting through my legs. I thought of sailors I knew actually having their legs snapped off.

It is deeper, darker, and then I am instantly above it all. I sees [sic] the ships. I sees [sic] the boats as they follow the whales. I sees [sic] the sun reflecting off the waves, all now gone.

JD: Feeling no pain and no undo emotion, let us begin the process of letting go. Why did you bring this fear and pain through time with you?

Joanna: I wanted to give my last pay to the woman I had my daughter by. The little girl is twelve, she is beautiful but sickly, and they live in a poor and cold house by the sea. It is what I have been going to sea for all these years. They won't get my pay because the captain will keep it.

Joanna can now go in the water. Although she is still afraid, she can approach the fear and get through it.

The effects of a karmic remnant may create more karma in this life. In some cases it can be helpful or necessary to consult a licensed, trained hypnotherapist or psychotherapist. Many individuals who act in an irrational manner may have a detrimental karmic remnant that has been triggered. A licensed hypnotherapist or psychotherapist can carefully take this individual back to the initial sensitizing experience and through a series of steps to help leave the remnant behind.

Next, a hypnotherapist recalls his work with a man who sought help in ridding himself of a karmic remnant, the fear of knives. This client was openly prejudiced; therefore, the concepts of diversity and reincarnation were difficult to digest.

The man regressed to a previous life in Africa. He was a noted warrior and a highly skilled fighter with a reputation for bravery. He decided he wanted the wife of one of the younger men in the tribe, but of course, the young man was not about to give her up. There was a challenge.

In his arrogance the warrior did not take the young man seriously. He went into the fight—a knife fight—feeling that it would be an easy victory. The young man evaded the great warrior and, with one slash, disemboweled him. The warrior caught his intestines in his hands and stood looking down at them in disbelief.

At this point in the regression, my client was becoming agitated and uncomfortable. I asked him to explain, without pain and without emotion, why he was becoming so agitated. He said, "I see this black face right in front of me. Now he holds the knife up to my nose and smiles and tells me that I should have given him more respect. He cuts my throat and I pass. I die and see the whole thing below."

I took him through the process of letting go of that incident. We worked on releasing the fear of knives while still respecting them.

When I brought him out of the regression, he stood and yelled at me, "You son of a bitch! What did you do to me? I could never be a black man!"

I replied that I had done nothing. He was the one telling the story, and I had the entire regression on tape, in his own words. I explained the reason for the story, the karmic remnant link between knives and attitudes.

I hope that he took this opportunity to gain insight into how we reincarnate in different forms — race, gender, and otherwise. Diversity is limitless.

---

*Examining past life behavior is a wonderful
way to promote an understanding of diversity,
for nothing is ever as it appears.*

Undiagnosed or ignored karmic remnants are not always tragic. Most manifest themselves merely as idiosyncrasies or mild phobias. Sometimes a karmic remnant can cause us to engage in negative behavior. The consequences of such behavior have to be righted in this life or a future incarnation. This can be achieved through a cosmic apology (reorganized lesson plans) or an added cycle of reincarnation.

Past-life regressions enable us to visit happier times or enjoy talents we do not presently possess. They can help us answer questions about relationships. When exploring your past lives you may find your memories differ from accepted accounts of history. Remember, history books are written by the victors and almost always show kings, princes, popes, and generals in the most favorable way possible, even to the point of fabrication.

*The past actually happened but history is only what
someone wrote down.* — *A. Whitney Brown*

Your Akashic Record

Each experience is a lesson that builds a better soul. The soul houses the cumulative knowledge of all of your lifetimes. This is your karma, your Akashic Record, your book of life. This earthly incarnation is a classroom. Incarnating on the earth plane accelerates our learning of these lessons. It is a privilege to be here, for every soul that has chosen to be here has the capacity to understand its purpose. Our choice to be here and the choices we make while we are here accelerate our path toward Spirit. Our choices affect the vibrations of the entire earth plane. The following past-life regression shows the efficiency of this earth plane as a classroom:

Susan: I have a pail in hand, going out to the barn. I am a girl, I am only eight, and I am going to the barn to milk the cow. The cats come running when they hear the milk pan rattle. They know they are going to get milk. There is only one cow. My name is Anna. I live in America.

JD: Do you have a last name?

Susan: No. Oh, yes. Wagner, Anna Wagner.

JD: Are your parents born in this country?

Susan: My father was not born in this country, but my mother was. My father was from Prussia, Germany. He speaks good English.

JD: Is he a farmer?

Susan: Yes.

JD: What year?

Susan: 1826.

JD: Do you have a brother or sister?

Susan: No, I don't see any around.

JD: Let's move ahead, a very important event after you are eight. See this with only joy.

Susan: I am 17, just getting married, moving farther west. I think I am in Ohio. That is where my farm is and my family live [sic]. My husband and I are going to Wyoming territory. My new husband has land out there. His brothers have gone out ahead, and they are all going to farm together.

JD: Tell the high points.

Susan: I have to say goodbye to my parents. I know I will

never see them again. It is sad for a couple of days. It is very hard.

We meet up with another family, and we travel together a few days down the road. We have to hurry because it is August and we have to get there before the heavy snows. Sometime in September the snows start. We have a covered wagon with just two mules and a dog, a big dog. We have a river to cross, and the men get together to figure out how to cross the river. It is not the real big river. One man wants to cross right here. My husband, Daniel, says to go on up the river to find a shallow place. We cross it here. We finally get to the other side. We travel for three more days. I am afraid of Indians, but we see none.

Finally, we get to our land. It seems the two brothers that went ahead got the better land. We have the poor soil. We have higher land, and they are in the valley. My husband is very angry. We stay there; he builds a cabin. The brothers help, but there is a lot of animosity. We try to farm but we can't. He gets some cattle. We start with a few steers, just two or three at a time. They die from some kind of a disease. He won't farm. He is pretty discouraged. We are very poor, but the brothers give us food—a lot of venison and a lot of rabbit.

JD: Any thought of going back or moving on?

Susan: He is tired; we will stay. I work, hoeing in the field. Winters are the worst, months inside. No children, just the two of us.

JD: Move on to another event. What's happening?

Susan: The feud between the three brothers has gotten worse; Daniel gets despondent, goes to bed, and never gets up again. He is the youngest brother.

JD: Your opinion of your husband?

Susan: Good man, but never wanted to better himself.

JD: What effect does that have on your life?

Susan: I've made up my mind that you do the best you can; you accept your own fate. If I were a man, I would move on and be responsible for my own actions.

JD: How old is he when he dies?

Susan: 38.

JD: How old are you when he dies?

Susan: 33.

JD: What happens to you now?

Susan: I stay there and the brothers take care of me. In three or four years a drummer comes along with his wagon. I have nothing; I just go with him. He makes a good living. Still have no children. He sells buttons, repairs pots and pans, knives, etc. We travel from homestead to homestead, Wyoming, Oregon. I always wanted to go to California, but it is too hard and he has steady customers. Steady life, but no children.

JD: Do you live longer than he, or do you pass first?

Susan: I don't see me by myself; I must die before he does.

JD: Let's go up to a few minutes before you die in that lifetime.

Susan: I am in a town, in a hotel room on the second floor, window open, curtain dirty, water black, wind blowing curtains, cardboard sign against window. I see 'Saloon' written on a sign across the street from the hotel. My husband is here sitting in the chair. I have a pain in my stomach, and I cough. I can't breathe. It is hard. I can't catch my breath. He holds my hand and I die. He is sad. He loved me very much, and he is alone. I was 45.

JD: What happens now?

Susan: I am going up and up. There are people there. I am in a classroom. Someone has me by the hand and leads me. I sit down at a bench. No emotions. I know these things have to be done, and I do them.

JD: What are they telling you?

Susan: They have different books, and they tell me these things. I can't read all the books, just what they give me. It is an examination of my life. I can only read what they tell me, and I cannot turn the pages. I do not know what it is, but they get another book. At the time it makes sense. I look at it, shake my head. Then they come over, close the book, put it back, and get another one. I must be studying.

JD: But it all seems right?

Susan: Yes.

JD: What happens next?

Susan: On the other side I make the decision to come back.

JD: I will count. Let's go to an exciting time, more adventuresome. One, two, three. You are there. What are you doing?

Susan: I am a sailor on board a ship, a whaling ship.

JD: How old?

Susan: 17 or so. I love it, the cold air.

What lessons did Susan learn from her lifetime as Anna? The overall impression is that she chose to learn lessons related to tolerance. Consider the free-will choices of others around her including her brothers-in-law. In farming the valley, what was their intent? Perhaps they had or were anticipating mouths to feed. Perhaps they felt they could not let good land go to waste while waiting for their brother.

What if Anna's first husband had been a hard worker and decided to move on rather than give up? What if she had children? What if she had been a man? The answers to these questions serve to show only the specific circumstances of this life. Her life as Anna formed a foundation for her future lives.

We examine our current lives and karmic paths without judgment or emotion, realizing our lives are interwoven with those of others.

Affirmation of Karma

Today I will see the life lessons that are offered to me by my actions, past and present. Today I choose to think before I act.

Prayer for Karma

Spirit, it is with a strong and generous heart that I bequest from You the strength and the power to objectively seek out the actions of others in order to begin, continue, and finish those processes I have begun so long ago. It is with joy promoted by the color orange that I bathe in Your love and evoke Your creative self within my own life and daily tasks. On this joyous day I step forth and thank You for interactions within my daily life. Thank You for my constant companions of earth, air, fire, water, and all creatures residing in this great garden You have called Earth. Amen.

CHAPTER THREE

wednesday

Universal Truth: *Purity*

Chakra: *Solar Plexus* ~ Color: *Yellow* ~ Number: *3*

Musical Keynote: *E*

Vocal Sound: *Short "O" as in "dog"*

Affirmation: *My thoughts create.*

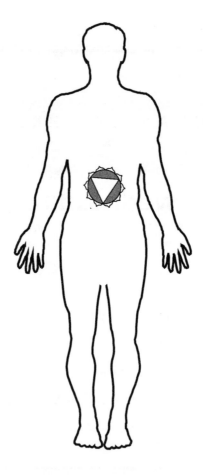

Chakra: *Solar Plexus*

You are matter. You do matter.
You make a difference
by simply being.

Purity is the third Universal Truth. The color yellow is a vibratory trigger for purity. Yellow has the highest visibility in the spectrum. The third chakra, or energy point, is known as the solar plexus. The number 3 vibrates to the Universal Truth of purity.

Purity is a state of being that we can attain just as we can attain the state of grace or the state of hope. Purity is the cleansing of the mind to allow room for a higher order and to cultivate understanding. Purity of action results from purity of thought.

We are the living thoughts of God.

In Christian tradition, Christ was pure in thought and deed. He was the example of how one may purify the body, mind, and spirit. He exemplified that thoughts are living things. He demonstrated that when we dismiss ego and move into the light, our thoughts are purified and our deeds soon follow. Christ talked of purity in many of his sermons and referred often to water and cleansing. Our bodies are comprised mostly of water and can purify and are purified. As the birthing waters break, we are born pure. If we become impure, we can cleanse ourselves. This transformation occurs through the cultivation of pure and positive thoughts that propel us toward our goals and happiness. Man is not what he thinks he is; he is what he thinks. Pure thoughts make man pure.

I think, therefore I am. —*René Descartes*

Yellow: The Color of Purity

Many of us think of purity as white or clear. Actually, the color associated with purity is yellow. Yellow is also the color of learning and ego. Purity of the mind, thought, and intellect leads to purity of action and then purity of the soul. Our thoughts are manifested in the environment we create through our actions. Likewise, our environment influences our thoughts, which in turn influence our actions.

The psychological qualities associated with yellow are organization, strong intellect and personality, discipline, knowledge, administration, and the ability to learn. Yellow is the color of career issues, analytical approaches, science, and political aspirations.

Yellow is advantageous to the nerves and brain. In color therapy, yellow light is projected around people who have psychological problems such as melancholy and depression or who feel tired of living. Yellow also helps eradicate fears and phobias.

Yellow has a positive effect on the digestive organs by stimulating the production of gastric juices and strengthening digestion. The liver and urinary system also benefit from yellow. Being surrounded with yellow is a good idea when dieting. It also can help with the regeneration of cells and the creation of emotional harmony. Like red, yellow increases blood pressure, pulse, and respiratory rates. Including yellow in your environment can help you obtain and maintain the state of purity.

Throughout your day:

- Notice yellow in your environment and how it affects you. Yellow stimulates the intellect. Are you writing with a yellow pencil or on a yellow note pad? Yellow is used to mark areas that involve risk. Is your awareness sharpened when you see yellow caution signs or tape? Where do you find yellow throughout your day?

- Project purity by wearing a shade of yellow fitting your personality. It may be a tie, undergarments, socks, jewelry, accessories, or an entire outfit.

- Drink out of a yellow glass or cup.

- Nourish your body with yellow foods.

- Charge your crystal with the power of yellow (see Chapter 9). This will help you reformulate your thoughts to become positive and affirming. Use this crystal to assist you in living in the present. The universe only recognizes what is. What will be always remains in the future! You are a success, you have abundance, and you are fulfilled.

3: The Number of Purity

The 3 vibration is the number for self-expression. Vibrating to the Universal Truth of purity, the numerological characteristics of the number are:

- Imaginative
- Visionary
- Happiness
- Celebration
- Political Aspirations

E: The Musical Keynote of Purity

The musical keynote of E is the auditory vibration for the Universal Truth of purity. If the key of E were visible, it would vibrate to the color of yellow. The vocal equivalent to the keynote of E is the short "O" sound as in "dog."

Understanding the Universal Truth of Purity

The human body is approximately two-thirds water. Each tiny drop is comprised of minute prisms that filter and project energy to all organs. This view helps us understand how we can bring about the purity of the soul through purity of thought and action. Through the effort of purifying our body, we purify our soul. When we purify ourselves, we influence the people around us in a positive manner, thus elevating the vibratory patterns of the entire earth plane.

You are matter. You do matter. You make a difference by simply being.

Life is real! Life is earnest!
And the grave is not its goal;
Dust thou art, to dust returnest,
Was not spoken of the soul.
—Henry Wadsworth Longfellow
(from "A Psalm of Life")

By understanding purity is a state of being, we can begin to live the Universal Truths. The body breathes. The body bathes. The body creates. What is in the mind can and will be manifested throughout lifetimes. When the body turns to ash, where does the crystalline structure of the water go? As it evaporates, it flows upward and becomes structures in yet another realm. Think of this each time you take a drink.

Water symbolizes purity.
The body is one vessel through which purity
flows; the soul is the other.

As we reincarnate and strive to learn our life lessons, we seek purity and perfection of our soul. Thoughts are living things that manifest themselves physically. The past-life regressions included in this chapter illustrate this relationship.

Maria developed indentations on her thighs during times of stress, particularly those situations dealing with men. She often projected dark and hateful thoughts toward these individuals and sought help at several clinics without relief. The hypnotherapist guided her to a stressful experience in a past life, which caused the indentations to reappear on her thighs during the session.

> *JD: What is happening at this time?*
>
> **Maria:** *My lover is leaving. I am following him to his carriage. I grab him; I am crying hysterically. 'Don't go! Don't go! I beg you!'*
>
> *JD: What is happening now?*
>
> **Maria:** *He has pushed me out of the way. My dress has become entangled in one of the carriage wheels.*
>
> *JD: Without undo emotion, please explain what is happening.*
>
> **Maria:** *The coach has run over my legs. The bones are not broken, but the flesh is mutilated.*

Maria goes on to describe the permanent damage done to her legs and her suffering from long-term chronic pain. She discovers she ended that life in suicide. The hypnotherapist tells her, while she is in a trance, to recognize that this event was another time and place and release it to the past. After the session the indentations disappear.

Maria goes on to learn stress management techniques and never has another incident. She learned you can change your past by changing how you think about your past, thus creating a positive future. Let history be kind to you!

What is in the mind can and will be manifested throughout lifetimes.

Bringing Out Purity

Your environment does not solely consist of light, color, music, and inanimate objects, but relationships as well. Purity is not just within you; it flows back and forth between you and the environment around you. It is important to create an environment that encourages purity. Surround yourself with items representing purity. It could be a calming water fountain, fresh flowers (even dandelions!), an inspiring work of art, or an aquarium. Create a clean, cleansing environment to assist you in achieving purity. Use yellow in decorating and dressing. Allow plenty of light into your life, both at home and at work. Play music featuring flutes, strings, and celestial themes. Mozart has been proven to stimulate thought. Listen to the laugh of a child. All of these are sensory cues, which are processed through the brain and act as vibratory triggers to purity. It is vital to support your purest thoughts with vibratory triggers.

Purity and Its Relationship to Health

Purity is a state allowing you to effectively interpret your life lessons. You may learn these lessons not just psychologically, but physically. Purity of attitude can bring healthful manifestations of life lessons, just as negativity and depression can create dis-ease. Striving for and achieving purity allow you to be aware and address your shortfalls. Illness can be a trigger leading us to respect our bodies. This realization can mean better health.

*You are more likely to be well if you attach
more importance to the living of your life rather
than to the illness you think defines you!*

As described in Chapter 1, karmic remnants are extraneous reverberations of karmic lessons already learned in a previous lifetime. There are many past-life regressions dealing with karmic remnants on issues of environment, nutrition, and health. Karmic remnants of this type all center around purity of thought and action.

> *What? know ye not that your body is the temple of the*
> *Holy Ghost [which is] in you, which ye have of God, and*
> *ye are not your own? For ye are bought with a price:*
> *therefore glorify God in your body, and in your spirit,*
> *which are God's.*
> *—1 Corinthians 6:19–20*

The following past-life regression was conducted with a client who was known to his colleagues and friends to be miserly. A teacher, he would send students to buy his cafeteria lunch, saving fifty cents. He would even turn his car off to coast down the hill toward his driveway to save gas. He was the butt of many jokes. This man suffered from asthma. Although he did not believe in reincarnation, he decided to be hypnotically regressed to see if it would help his asthma.

> *JD: Where are you, and what year is it?*
>
> *Mark: [proudly] Egypt. It is the second year of the reign of Ramses the Second!*
>
> *JD: What do you do?*
>
> *Mark: [again, proudly] I am a merchant.*
>
> *JD: What type of merchant?*
>
> *Mark: I import leathers and hides from Black Africa.*
>
> *JD: What they are [sic] used for?*
>
> *Mark: The temples use them often, but others use them as*

a social statement and proudly show these exotic skins. I have two sons in the business with me.

JD: Let your higher self answer this question: What does this life in Egypt have to do with your asthma?

Mark: The hides and skins need to be cleaned and prepared after transport across the desert. Some hides also need to be tanned. The processes we use have hurt my lungs.

JD: Let us move to the time of your death. How do you feel?

Mark: Angry.

JD: Why?

Mark: My two sons have taken the wealth that I have accumulated, which is to be buried with me for use on the other side, and traded it for junk from the bazaar. I will be buried with less than I deserve!

JD: Let us return to the present. Does this incident explain why you are so frugal in this life?

Mark: Yes. I intend to keep what is rightfully mine.

JD: I can see that you have held on to much from that lifetime, including the anger and breathing problems. Now that you can see what has happened, you can, as I count slowly to ten, let go of these negative things from the past that now are needlessly hurting you. Let the subconscious mind work its way through this problem, and when it is resolved, hold your right hand up.

Mark: [very quickly raises right hand]

Following this session, Mark told John Dull his asthma attacks were greatly reduced in frequency and severity. This regression brought understanding and therefore changed his attitude.

The Ease of Purity

Learning lessons does not have to be painful. Lessons can be learned through abundance and joy. Purity is the foundation for learning and understanding all our life lessons. The objectives of our life lessons become clear when purity is achieved. Purity becomes a companion and provides synergistic assistance for the processing of each Universal Truth and life lessons.

Reformulate the beliefs that have limited you and replace them with limitless aspirations.

Affirmation of Purity

Today I am aware that my own thoughts and attitudes, along with those of others, are living things. Through pure thoughts and the pure actions they produce, I can create my own positive, wonderful, and abundant life.

Prayer for Purity

Spirit, I ask for objectivity in my daily routines and for the ability to see through others' eyes, in order to understand their initiatives on this earth plane. Purity begins through cleansing of the mind, body, and spirit. This triad comes into perfect unity as I breathe in the yellow light of purity. With each breath I allow myself to hold Your light and love and begin my journey back to Your divine energy with a pure mind, body, and spirit. Amen.

CHAPTER FOUR

thursday

Universal Truth: *Love*

Chakra: *Heart* ~ Color: *Green* ~ Numbers: *4, 9*

Musical Keynote: *F*

Vocal Sound: *"Ah"*

Affirmation: *I embrace all relationships*
with compassion and love.

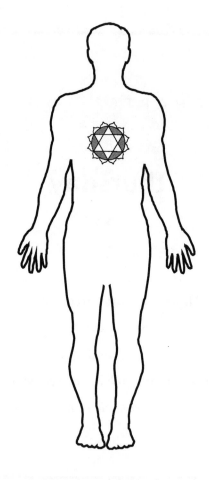

Chakra: *Heart*

Love is in all relationships.
It begins within you.

Love is the fourth Universal Truth. The color green is the vibratory trigger for love. The fourth chakra, or energy point in the body, is known as the heart chakra. The numbers 4 and 9 vibrate to this Universal Truth.

Love is an embraceable emotion. The heart is often associated with the color red, the color of passion, but the heart chakra is green, cool and healing in its intentions. Humans experience many different kinds of love—the love of family, nature, self, and Spirit. Love may take on different forms when guided by male or female energy. Female energy tends to express love through nurturing, while male energy tends to express love through provision. This is not to say they do not initially relay love in the same manner. It is a matter of reception. There are frequent misunderstandings regarding love in relationships because love is sent out with the same intent by both energies, yet can be received differently.

Inherently, human energy will muster and send forth love with the same intentions. Their receptors pick up different vibratory frequencies, and misinterpretations follow. What is the difference between the "hunter" and the "gatherer"? Do they not both provide? Is instinct in the intent behind the action, or is instinct in the final result? As providers, male and female energies nurture. The division is not in the intent. The division is in the *interpretation* of the intent.

Vibratory frequencies act as a cloak, which should be compared to the nakedness of Adam and Eve. In Christian tradition, Adam and Eve did not encounter conflict until choice (red) was introduced, accompanied by free will and karma. This occurred when Eve and then Adam ate the "forbidden" fruit. After this, choice and consequences were thrust upon them. When free will manifested, so did conditional love. They recognized they were different and hid themselves from God and from each other. It is the beginning of relationships. It is the beginning of love.

The Garden of Eden was a garden of lush green beauty. It was fruitful and plentiful in its offerings. Green is new beginnings. It is love and relationships. It is healing. It is teaching. Adam and Eve cohabitated in perfect harmony before free will. They did not have conditions placed on image or actions. Before free will and karma were introduced through choice, there was no separation of the chakras. Balance and harmony existed between the energies.

Thursday is a day to examine relationships between you, others, and Spirit. Encompassing the lessons learned for free will, karma, and purity, think about how you nurture and provide for others and yourself. Thursday is the day to realize anything is achievable when you nurture and maintain a positive and loving relationship with yourself. It is the day to begin the practice of saying, "I love myself!"

As you go through your day, recognize the positive aspects of the activities you perform. It is a great gift to the universe to love yourself. The universe honors and rewards this!

Pay attention to your relationships with objects, nature, and humans. Do not limit your relationships. Everything is possible when you love yourself. Recognize that you deserve to love and be loved.

One word frees us of all the weight and pain of life:
That word is love. — Sophocles

Green: The Color of Love

Green generates new growth and beginnings. It represents the nurturing of a relationship with self, others, and the universe. No relationship can flourish until one is true to self. Green is harmony and combines the warmth of yellow (intellect and self) with the coolness of blue (truth and loyalty). Green is the bridge between the three warm earthly colors and the three cool spiritual colors and is the bridge between heaven and earth. Green is the color of teaching. It is calming for individuals and allows them to absorb information and process it accordingly.

In color therapy, green is used to treat shock, calm headaches, and relieve stress from daily activities. It also aids in memory recall. Green is a healing color associated with the healing arts. Many hospitals incorporate a green tint on interior walls to help calm patients. Surgical scrubs are green to help alleviate eye fatigue during long procedures. However, green should be used with caution in healing because it stimulates growth.

In society, green is associated with money. It fosters an awareness of existing opportunities. Green generates prosperity and fertility. It is the color of grass, new foundations, and bright, positive beginnings.

Using the color green in your personal environment will bring about a willingness to approach situations with understanding and compassion. It fosters mediation in conflict. Green brings about emotional and mental clarity. It helps achieve the best possible results for any task we decide to execute. Think about how green is present in all relationships in your life. These relationships will allow you to engage in the mutual learning of life lessons.

Throughout your day:

- Wear green, seen or unseen.

- Each time you see a reflection of yourself, make it a point to say unconditionally, "I Love Me!"

- Honor and thank your money and arrange it in order. Charge it with love and send that positive message on to others. Pay your debts, sending spiritual thanks to your creditors for trusting you. Discard the distaste of owing and rejoice in the trust of lending!

- Eat your veggies. Green vegetables aid physical stamina and provide the roughage needed for detoxification.

- When you look outside, scan for green. Feel the difference when you walk on grass, touch a leaf, or water the plant in your office. Even dusting the silk leaves on the plant that never dies helps attune you to the loving power of green.

• Charge your crystal with the power of green. (For instructions, turn to Chapter 9). Ask it to help you pay attention to your role of "teacher" today. What lessons are you teaching?

4, 9: The Numbers of Love

The 4 vibration is the number for building foundations. Vibrating to the Universal Truth of love, the numerological characteristics of the number 4 are:

• Self-discipline

• Construction

• Foundations

• Family

• Seriousness

• Drama

The 9 vibration is for the humanitarian. The numerological characteristics of the number 9 are:

• Unconditional Love

• Brotherhood

• Forgiveness

• Ideality

• Endings

• Completion

F: The Musical Keynote of Love

The musical keynote of F is the correct auditory vibration for the Universal Truth of love. If the key of F were visible, it would vibrate to the color of green. The vocal equivalent to the key of F is the "ah" sound.

Understanding the Universal Truth of Love: Unconditional Love

In Christian tradition, the love that existed between Adam and Eve and the world of Eden was a love unconditional. With the "fall" of Adam and Eve and the introduction of free will came the loss of unconditional love. We have been striving to achieve this perfect state ever since.

Although we say we understand what the meaning of unconditional love is, we cannot attain this by merely understanding. It does not embrace any other human or soul; it is a state that is purely individual. When this state is reached, we retain the choice to join the Divine Creator as an "Individual Whole" embracing love unconditional. We may also choose to retain our own individual self, residing in harmony with the Divine Creator and circling the orbit—harmonic yet still individually recognized.

When we are engaged in unconditional love, we are neither complacent nor apathetic. Pure harmony, created by processing unconditional love, is ecstasy. It is the final step in becoming one with Spirit.

Emotion

Unconditional love is the pure energy of the universe. It is nirvana, heaven, and the hereafter. It is harmonic perfection. Unconditional love is the balance of energy, color, and light. The perfect harmony of unconditional love brings about full enlightenment. Emotion holds us to the earth plane. Unconditional love is achieved as we begin to shed earthly physicality and leave emotion behind.

Mother Earth and the life residing with her have retained the memory of unconditional love in order to remind us of our humble beginnings. Because of this, small children, the earth, animals, and plant life have vibrational triggers that remind us of what we have forgotten and help us to rekindle the journey toward the Divine. There is an unexplained and deep loathing for those who mistreat children, babies, and animals; desecrate Mother Earth; and have little regard for any of the inhabitants. This emotional reaction is a subconscious cry to not abandon our roots. If we ignore or silence our disgust, we will lose our way.

Gender and Attraction

Confusion and misunderstanding exist where love and masculine/feminine relationships are concerned. Perhaps it begins with Noah and the ark, two by two. Perhaps it is with the mating ritual overall. Numerologically the number two vibrates to relationships. The Universal Truth of love vibrates to green, and it is the fourth chakra (two by two). Four, in and of itself, deals with drama and dramatic relationships. More importantly, relationships are opposing, and to have an opposition, one must have two. Opposites attract; that is the law of polarity.

Attraction is different from unconditional love. Attraction is dependent on the brain, mind, and hormonal triggers. Feminine energy is *emotion;* masculine energy is *logic.* This is the yin and yang of attraction. In this sense, opposites do attract. The feminine approach to relationships is from an emotional standpoint. The masculine approach to relationships is from a practical standpoint.

Human Love Versus Unconditional Love

Often, the expressions "true love" and "soul mate" are used. True love is a balancing of the senses. It results in what humans see as a perfect fit with a soul mate. This kind of love is completely human—the love we dream about, write about, and sing about. Conversely, unconditional love originates from neither the emotions nor the brain nor the body.

Each of our bodies is made up of molecules that vibrate at certain frequencies. The vibratory frequency leads us to be attracted to some people and unattracted to others. Think of your body as a ball of liquid mercury on a platter. Another ball of mercury is placed at the other end of the platter, and the platter is tilted. Your body rolls toward the other body, and when they come into contact, they cannot be stopped from merging.

Unlike human love, there is no physical or emotional aspect to unconditional love. Human romantic love is a sexual and emotional love. It is attraction caused by the vibratory atoms within the body. Certain scents excite. Certain energy colors attract. These are chemical reactions. There is a definite physical response that can be measured with instruments and physically observed. The sexual act amasses two beings' energies and is often mistakenly confused with love. Unconditional love is a love beyond such reactions.

Soul Mate

Soul mate is a term that conveys the intense emotion of human love for another individual. Love for a soul mate is conditional, but nevertheless it may be deep and at times inexplicable. It approaches unconditional love, for it is a love between souls that goes beyond human boundaries. However, a relationship with a soul mate more often than not has a sexual component and is confined to human constructs. In truth, there is no one person who is your destined mate for eternity. There is no soul mate. A better term for this is "path partner".

Path Partner

A *path partner,* by contrast, is a soul with whom you are comfortable and familiar. You have made a contract to be together in this lifetime to help each other learn life lessons. Those lessons need not center on personal relationships. You are on the same evolutionary plane and the same path toward spiritual development. Think about the person you are with. You met and knew that you would be together. That is the contract. Many path partners repeat lifetimes together.

You may have several path partners, as do those who experience divorce; the partners teach each other a life lesson and then move on. You may have a period in which you have no path partner because you need to work on a personal issue individually. Meeting and being with your path partner does not mean you are done learning about personal relationships. You have a partner because you learn more lessons together than you would apart.

Kindred Spirit

Kindred spirits represent another kind of conditional love. Kindred spirits can be a girl and her best friend, a boy and his grandfather, a pupil and his mentor, etc. There is a predetermined bond between these souls. That bond may form only in passing, such as a chance meeting, a business encounter, even a miscarriage or stillbirth. These energies meet, creating a lasting impression and providing the opportunity for soul growth.

---

*The most important aspect of love is self-love.
In loving yourself and having a true relationship
with yourself, you bring about all of the truths
and the understanding of Spirit.*

Each lesson we learn in this and other lifetimes brings us closer to understanding unconditional love. When we have learned enough lessons, when we have been purified, when we understand unconditional love, then we will vibrate with the same frequency as Spirit. We will then be assumed into Spirit's mass and will be one.

This is heaven.

Affirmation of Love

Today I will examine all relationships. I will nurture new relationships. I will not take any relationship for granted. I will examine the benefits of my connections with colleagues, family members, Mother Earth, and the animals and plants that reside on earth with me. I will envelop my community, my family, and myself in the green light of love.

Prayer for Love

Spirit, I ask that the green light of love create harmony and balance within my body. It is this light that enables me to understand the true meaning of love. I ask for loving energy to be sent out to the earth. Help me appreciate the guides I encounter spontaneously throughout my lifetimes. I give thanks to You, Spirit, for the partnerships provided for me to learn my life lessons. Grant peace in my heart and grant the entire world love. Amen.

CHAPTER FIVE

friday

Universal Truth: *Truth*

Chakra: *Throat* ~ Color: *Blue* ~ Number: *5*

Musical Keynote: *G*

Vocal Sound: *"Eh"*

Affirmation: *I understand the intent*

behind an action.

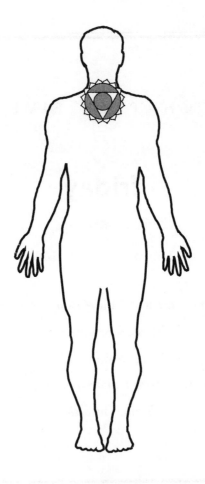

Chakra: *Throat*

Eyes are windows to the soul.
Truth is the gatekeeper.

Truth is the fifth Universal Truth. The color blue is a vibratory trigger for truth. The fifth chakra, or energy point in the body, is known as the throat chakra. The number 5 vibrates to this Universal Truth. For many, Friday is the last day of the workweek. Representing freedom, Friday is a day to begin activities for your weekend (when the five o'clock whistle blows).

Truth is a condition reached when one is aware of one's self and fully connected with others. It is this emotional connection of being truthful that is so important. We open ourselves to learning and helping others learn life lessons by offering to each other the feelings and thoughts we know to be true.

Blue: The Color of Truth

This color represents loyalty, integrity, and honor, as well as communication. Blue is a calm color. It is conducive to creative endeavors such as writing, art, and music. A room flooded with blue light has a calming effect, can reduce fever, and can ease the transition of the terminally ill.

In color therapy, blue is used to treat ailments of the throat and neck, including the thyroid and parathyroid glands. It is also used in treatments involving the upper respiratory system and aids in weight gain.

Blue is the color of business. IBM is one of the best-known corporations in the world and uses blue as its signature color. It is nicknamed "Big Blue." Advertisers use blue to sell health products and any item or idea that can be promoted through an emphasis on truth.

Blue attracts and projects loyalty. The blue suit instills trust during business dealings. It conveys honesty, professionalism, and sophistication. Blue translates as "You can trust me." The presence of blue assures communication is at an optimal level.

Using the color blue in your environment brings out these attributes. It can promote diligence, success, and a sense of accomplishment.

In situations where you need to think before you speak, it is wise to make blue a permanent fixture.

Throughout your day:

- Wear blue, seen or unseen. Blue clothing or accessories serve as a reminder to notice the truth in your actions.

- Notice blue in your environment, including advertisements and packaging. Who is wearing blue today?

- Drink out of a blue mug or cup.

- Charge your crystal with the power of blue (see Chapter 9). Using your crystal, examine what is presented as the truth rather than simply assume it is the truth.

- Identify positive attributes in people and compliment them. It may be as simple as noticing someone's pleasant smile or pleasant voice. He or she will perhaps pass the lesson on to others.

- Pay attention to the various forms of non-verbal communication by noticing gestures, expressions, and other body language.

- Open your arms, soak in blue sky, and ask that your true path be revealed to you.

5: The Number of Truth

The 5 vibration is the number for freedom and versatility. Vibrating to the Universal Truth of truth, the numerological characteristics of 5 are:

- Progressiveness
- Life Experience
- Action
- New Ideas

G: The Musical Keynote of Truth

The musical keynote of G is the correct auditory vibration for the Universal Truth of truth. If the key of G were visible, it would vibrate to the color of blue. The vocal equivalent to the key of G is the "eh" sound.

Understanding the Universal Truth of Truth

Truth is not about lies. It is not about measuring. Truth is about accessing the gifts of the universe. Truth, like beauty, is often in the eyes of the beholder. Truth always remains constant.

> *O, what a tangled web we weave,*
> *when first we practise to deceive!*
> *— Sir Walter Scott*

Truth and Intent

Truth, whether it is spoken or written, is wrapped in intent. Truth requires your voice to be heard. Christ was "the Truth" because he spoke the truth. He taught us how to pray. His words communicated the power of free will and karmic intent.

Gateway to the Akashic Records

Truth is the gate to the Akashic Records. It is the key to the kingdom. With truth, intent is made to show its hand. The physical plane allows us to hide the truth from each other if we choose. There is no hiding of the truth on the spiritual plane because there is not a physical body to mask intent. Eyes are windows to the soul. Truth is the gatekeeper. Look into the eyes when the truth is being sought. The pupil will dilate when the body is deceiving. The heart rhythm changes, and the voice of the throat chakra may even wane.

We exercise free will when we speak the truth and tell untruths. It is not about being unfaithful, but about being untruthful with your actions in order to avoid a negative reaction. When telling untruths there is a chemical reaction that takes place. Endorphins rage. It is a thrill to be untruthful and think one has gotten away with deceit. Falsehoods are as addictive as gambling and other vices of the emotions. Pathological liars believe their own lies. They can assimilate lies into their own existence by justifying their behavior for the greater good. Truth, however, is the natural way of the universe. We are dependent on truth to guide us on our journey of learning life lessons.

Eyes are windows to the soul.
Truth is the gatekeeper.

Truth is your soul getting down to business. When the cosmic laws are not followed, physical triggers are tripped. The sympathetic nervous system is stimulated, causing an increase in heart rate, respirations, and perspiration. Lie detectors utilize these physical changes in the human body. Sometimes we can perceive these changes and sense someone is being dishonest. It is important to contemplate the intent of our interactions with those around us and ask if we are being truthful. They say the devil is in the details; actually, God is in the details. There has to be truth in the details in order to find God.

On the physical plane, we may choose to hide the truth from each other. On the other side there is no hiding. There is no physical body to mask intent. The Akashic Records hold our true intent. These entries are neither good nor bad. They are simply truthful. The truth is the vital source for the Akashic Records. This understanding frees us to be guided by the truth. Truth is a pivotal Universal Truth.

Faith is belief without foundation.
Truth is the foundation of belief.

The following true story illustrates how being attuned to the truth can radically change our lives and put us on the path of our life lessons:

Keith's father was once a football star at the state university and is now a successful businessman. Keith is athletic and participated in sports, but had not been a star. His first love was art, at which he was quite talented. Keith wanted desperately to please his father, who believed artistic men were "wusses," so he kept his drawings to himself. Keith married the daughter of a friend of his father. He went to work for his father-in-law as an architect and constantly reminded himself architecture was an art form.

Keith was miserable and only became more so when he learned his wife was having an affair with an old boyfriend. In return, Keith had several one-night stands, making him feel guilty. He continued to feel simmering resentment toward his wife. Professionally, he felt underused and devalued, and his domineering father and father-in-law were driving him to despair. Keith began to experience stress and anxiety attacks. His family doctor prescribed antidepressants and also suggested self-hypnosis as a form of relaxation therapy.

The hypnotherapist explained that while he could indeed teach Keith self-hypnosis for relaxation, it wouldn't resolve the causes of his stress. Hypnosis was used to open Keith's subconscious mind to reveal more about what was causing his stress.

> *JD: What is the cause of the stress you are feeling?*
> *Keith: [tearfully] I'm living a lie, a giant lie. Everything in my life is a lie.*
> *JD: What will resolve this living a lie?*

Keith: To thine own self be true. The truth shall set you free [Repeated three times].

JD: How does that translate into your own life?

Keith: I may not be able to get rid of my dad—I love him, but I can't stand him. I can move away, and I can become free of my unfaithful wife, her father, and the job. I can do something to make me proud and happy, doing what I really want to do, being who I think I really am.

Upon concluding the trance, the hypnotherapist did not instruct Keith to forget what had happened during the session. Keith remembered the regression on the conscious level and emerged from his trance looking surprised.

The next Christmas the hypnotherapist received a hand-painted card from Keith, who is now living in another state. He wrote that he was happy, free, and living his truth.

Affirmation of Truth

Today I will seek to be receptive to the truths others may share with me. I will not judge. I will be honest, loyal, and truthful in my interactions with others and myself. Friday is the day to go beyond hearing. I will listen, keenly observing the truth behind words and actions.

Prayer for Truth

Spirit, I ask You to open all my senses and bring forth the willingness to seek out the truth in my everyday life. Help me as I seek truth in every detail. I look for goodness in all. I pray that as I move through this day, I may recognize the truth in others, including Mother Earth, and the truth in myself. It is with the intent to learn the lessons You have placed before me that I fully embrace truth. Amen.

CHAPTER SIX

saturday

Universal Truth: *Faith*

Chakra: *Third Eye* ~ Color: *Indigo* ~ Number: *6*

Musical Keynote: *A*

Vocal Sound: *"Ee"*

Affirmation: *I recognize the positive*

qualities in everyone.

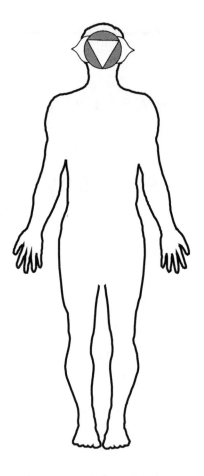

Chakra: *Third Eye*

Your dreams are divine faith.
Wrap them in affirmation.

Faith is the sixth Universal Truth. The color indigo is a vibratory trigger for faith. The sixth chakra, or energy point in the body, is known as the third eye. It vibrates in accordance with indigo and faith. The number 6 vibrates to this Universal Truth.

Faith is a great ally to those who possess it. Faith gives us hope and joy. It frees us from the pain and anguish of death. Faith does not change a situation; it changes our perception of the situation. Rather than say, "Woe is me; what will I do?" we should say, "I don't like what happened, but it will lead to something better."

Faith is the belief that something is without knowing why. It provides the confidence we need to pursue an undertaking. Hope is the trust and knowledge that a higher realm of guidance exists. Faith is the knowing and trusting of self. Faith is in knowing that you have orchestrated your life's path well and you can take that next leap forward in life. Faith is knowing you built that leap into a particular chapter of the book we call "Your Life."

---

*Faith is the belief that something **is** without knowing **why**.*

Indigo: The Color of Faith

Faith is associated with the color indigo. Indigo activates intuition. It is the color located in the third eye region. It represents the skeletal system, the foundation of the body.

Indigo and violet are associated with artists and those solitary souls searching for a cause. The undertones of red in the color violet set the personal journey into motion. When the journey has commenced, individuals tend to settle into the deep, calming comfort of indigo. Indigo communicates willpower and commitment. Anyone can use the energy of indigo to aid them as they perform their tasks.

Indigo governs the third eye region, which relates to the sinus cavities, eyes, pituitary gland, and lower brain. Indigo objects pull in the deepest rays of healing blue and create a catalyst for self-examination. Indigo promotes emotional healing and has a broad application in the healing process.

In color therapy, indigo is used to treat internal infections and inflammation. Its calming effect lowers the heartbeat, which creates a quiet, meditative state. This allows synchronization between the intuitive side and the physical body. Yellow is the complement of indigo and is used to treat psychological problems such as depression. Overexposure to indigo can trigger psychological problems.

Throughout your day:

- Wear indigo. Brand-new blue jeans are the most common place to find indigo in casual wardrobes.

- Drink out of an indigo glass or cup.

- Nourish your body with the steady flow of indigo energy by drinking grape juice and eating grapes, eggplant, plums, and other foods of this color.

- Place indigo accessories in your work environment. This can ease eyestrain, enable you to focus on your purpose, and nurture negotiation and mediation.

- Charge your crystal with the power of indigo (see Chapter 9) and ask yourself what recent events have involved faith. Recognize and listen to your inner voice of intuition.

6: The Number of Faith

The 6 vibration is the number of harmony and concern for others. Vibrating to the Universal Truth of faith, the numerological characteristics of this number are:

- Balance

- Service

- Family

- Nurturer

A: The Musical Keynote of Faith

The musical keynote of A is the auditory vibration for the Universal Truth of faith. If the key of A were visible, it would vibrate to the color of indigo. The vocal sound associated with the keynote of A is "ee."

Understanding the Universal Truth of Faith

It is never too late to generate faith. It begins with looking around yourself to see what aesthetics (color, music, numbers) you are drawn to. Analyzing this information will help you identify the lessons you have put before yourself. This is intuition at work. All knowledge is accessible. Ignorance flourishes when you choose not to question the existence of facts.

There is faith when you trust. Where do you place your trust? Place trust in your inner knowing and guidance, and trust that you have set up all the appropriate plans for the lessons to be learned. Have faith that you will orchestrate situations you have contracted to encounter with certain incarnated souls. In doing so, you help them with their lessons. As this occurs, you are completing your lessons and moving to the next challenge. In this capacity you are a soldier, tackling a lesson and moving on to the next challenge.

Discovering Faith

Your faith is your path to follow. You have all of the guidance you could ask for as you journey down this path. Guidance comes in many forms, such as advice from a friend or the hunch to drive home the long way. It can also be far more orchestrated and thorough than happenstance. Your initial indoctrination into faith is from parental guidance, then teachers, workers, and mentors. Your faith is the path that sustains your joy. Follow joy, for abundance awaits.

Mankind needs a body of beliefs for day-to-day security. We need faith in our spiritual existence, faith not threatened by damning hell or the promise of heavenly rewards. Faith is belief in spiritual existence without factual foundation, nothing more and nothing less.

Some may argue that they have taken the hard road, pressing ahead with diligence, not faith. However, they were able to overcome the obstacles on that road because they believed they could do so. They had faith that these obstacles could not stop them.

Faith and Religion

Religion is accumulated rituals consisting of spiritual concepts. Religious traditions evoke religious beliefs. Religious belief is the path presented for you to follow. Faith is the path you create for yourself. Faith is deeper and more personal than religion.

Religious belief is the path presented for you to follow. Faith is the path you create for yourself.

Although faith is not based on a religious tenet, it can be part of any religion. There are people who accept religion without thought, having been born into it. Others have changed religious affiliations to suit their beliefs. Still others are not part of any organized religion. In all of these cases, there is room for faith in our lives. It is common to adapt religion or atheistic philosophies to accommodate personal faith. Although religious belief is often equated with a church, faith is without an edifice. Faith is personal; each person carries it within.

Faith: Who Needs It?

Faith comes into play every day. When a company has broken faith, employees' morale and productivity plummet. A sports team without faith in the coach's system or game plan is seldom a winning team. Those with faith, however, are a formidable force.

When struggling with faith in your life, talking with the elderly in nursing homes can help you identify lessons in faith. Heartwarming stories of overcoming obstacles and illness are there for those who will listen. The stories of World War II veterans and women who ventured from home to the workplace illustrate the marriage of faith and hope. Faith is the path. Hope is the guidepost.

The Universal Truth of faith is the personal journey you have charted in order to learn and teach life lessons.

Faith has profound implications when we face death. People cling to life with a desperate fear of the unknown. They fear being judged for their sins and their lack of faith. This fear is unfounded because faith led them down this path. Do not judge yourself for lack of faith. Judge yourself on the intent behind the action, not the outcome. Faith brought you to this point of decision. Hope is what guides you to listen. Understand, the Universal Truth of faith is the personal journey you have charted in order to learn and teach life lessons.

Where Have You Been All Your Life?

Shorty and I were enjoying a cup of coffee and swapping jokes when Ernie joined us at the table. Ernie was about eighty years old. After sitting down he waited for Shorty to finish his joke. Ernie then asked if we believed in the hereafter.

I thought it was the opening line for another joke, but he was serious. We both answered in the affirmative. He responded by asking if we thought we would see our mothers there. Again, we said yes. His next question was, "How will they know who you are? You don't look much like you did when they died. You're old now. How will you see her when your eyeballs are back on earth in a hole in the ground?"

I was amazed at his take on the hereafter. This man had certainly attended the funerals of many friends and relatives over the years. Had he never thought about such things as what happens after the soul leaves the body? Had he never been exposed to any form of religious or spiritual ideas? How fearful it must be to not have faith or a belief system to guide you.

Suicide: A Crisis of Faith

Suicide involves a crisis of faith and is a serious violation of Universal Law. Souls, before they incarnate, are brave and ambitious. They may elect to take on loads of karma too large to balance in a single lifetime. Some souls choose to exercise free will by using suicide as a way of resolving this overload or what seems to be an impenetrable complex of problems. Faith allows us to see our problems as opportunities to learn life lessons. We learn those lessons over the course of lifetimes. No one is ever punished because a lesson was not learned.

Those who have committed suicide immediately reincarnate. They will have the same lessons to learn in order to move toward their soul perfection. The lessons arise in different orders from soul to soul, yet the lessons are the same for all of us. Those who commit suicide are not condemned to a burning hell. They will again be presented with the same opportunities to finish these lessons.

*Faith is a divine tool. It provides our goals,
our joys, and our aspirations.*

Faith Enables Joy

Imagine yourself as a tiny baby coming into the world with the conscious awareness of the sum total of all of the experiences of your past lives. The burden of consciously knowing all of the encounters and experiences you must face in this lifetime in order to fulfill your contract would be overwhelming.

Allowing us to be born with only a subconscious memory of the past is Spirit's way of letting us participate in our own creation. We learn the elements of faith and develop a workable belief system for ourselves. Because we are not burdened with the conscious awareness of past lives, we are able to experience joy in the learning.

Faith is a divine tool. It provides our goals, our joys, and our aspirations. Faith will lead you to your path, the path that generates and sustains your joy. Follow joy, for abundance awaits you! Your dreams are divine faith. Wrap them in affirmation.

Affirmation of Faith

Today I will assume the best about everyone. I will believe without question the inherent goodness of my family, friends, and community. I will spend this day knowing goodness within and emanating goodness throughout all aspects of my life.

Prayer for Faith

Spirit, I rejoice in the complete faith You have bestowed upon me so that I may continue to follow my path of joy and completeness. I ask that I be able to continue to recognize the guidance You offer as I glide from one success to another. I thank You for the courage to embrace my faith, understand my beliefs, and recognize the hope that surrounds me. My path is a path of joy, with faith and hope as my partners. Amen.

CHAPTER SEVEN

sunday

༄

Universal Truth: *Hope*

Chakra: *Crown* ~ Color: *White* ~ Number: 7

Musical Keynote: *B*

Vocal Sound: *"Ohm"*

Affirmation: *I receive guidance. I provide guidance.*

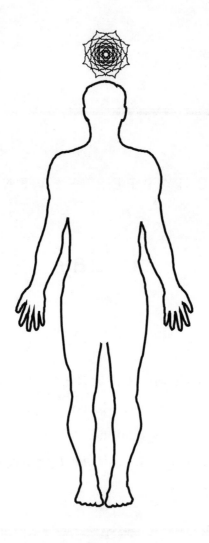

Chakra: *Crown*

Remember, you are never alone.

Help is only a thought away.

Hope is the seventh Universal Truth. The color white is a vibratory trigger for hope. The seventh chakra, or energy point in the body, is known as the crown chakra. The number 7 vibrates to this Universal Truth.

Hope that is seen is not hope: for what a man seeth, why doth he yet hope for? But if we hope for that we see not, [then] do we with patience wait for [it]. —**Romans 8:24–25**

The word hope is often used to convey the desire for things we do not possess. This is not hope. Hope occurs when we hold something in our minds and our hearts simultaneously. It is the convergence of love and belief. We may think we have hope contained in a neat little package. In fact, hope is everything outside the package. Without hope, there is nothing. We need hope in order to learn, grow, and evolve. It allows us to imagine possibilities and feed our dreams. Hope promotes thought. With thought comes manifestation. We experience hope when we trust guidance that is coming from a higher realm. To ask for this guidance is to embrace hope.

Hope is the convergence of love and belief.

White: The Color of Hope

White is the color of divine light. It encompasses all colors of the spectrum. White can take on many characteristics and can bring out the best in all colors. When we add white to a color, we get a pastel. That conversion can be interpreted as adding hope to the qualities associated with the original color. For example, red represents passion, heat, change, and quick energy. Bathe it in the divine light of white and you have pink. Pink represents the gentle, hopeful aspect of red, a passion that nurtures and spiritually transforms. We wrap babies in pastels to surround them with hope.

White is beneficial in a healing environment. A trend has emerged in recent years with health care professionals dressing in multi-colored patterns rather than the traditional white uniforms. Patients would benefit from shifting the trend back to white. When the nurse walks into the room, the patient responds to the full spectrum of white, drawing in the color he/she needs to balance the body and promote healing.

Hope is the dream of a waking man. —Aristotle

Throughout your day:

- Wear white, seen or unseen.
- Drink milk.
- Drink out of a white glass or cup.
- When you want to project healing thoughts, use white. The recipient will draw the colors most needed from the divine white light.
- White will accelerate all colors. Notice how divine white light sets stained glass into motion.
- Place your clear quartz crystal charged with the white light of hope (see Chapter 9) on your crown chakra and open yourself to Spirit.

7: The Number of Hope

The 7 vibration is the number for wisdom and inner self. The numerological characteristics of this number are:

- Knowledge
- Research

• Meditation

• Discovery

B: The Musical Keynote of Hope

The musical keynote of B is the correct auditory vibration for the Universal Truth of hope. If the keynote of B were visible, it would vibrate to white. The vocal equivalent to the keynote of B is "oh."

Understanding the Universal Truth of Hope

Hope is on an entirely different vibratory level. Hope is of the ethereal level. Hope is not something you can dream about or imagine. That is wish. Wish and hope, although brothers, are not the same. Wish is the earthly aspect of hope. Hope is the spiritual aspect of wish. Desire is the far more material form of wish.

Hope should not be seen within the context of wanting. That has been misinterpreted for generations upon generations. Master Jesus Christ was indeed "the Hope of the World." He brought a spiritual aspect to mankind. He personified hope by bringing intuitive, emotional, and spiritual guidance. Christ represented the unconditional surrender to heavenly guidance in order to illustrate for us how to exercise our free will and fulfill our karmic path.

Wish and hope, although brothers, are not the same. Wish is the earthly aspect of hope. Hope is the spiritual aspect of wish. Desire is the far more material form of wish.

Hope is involved in the final evolution of the soul as it reaches Spirit. When this evolution takes place, we accept that we have been put here as individuals, for we are solely responsible for the decisions that bring about our own evolution. Guidance has been and always will be there for us. It will encompass all of the possibilities that lie ahead. This guidance exists, allowing us to initiate, evaluate, and then negotiate the choices at hand. We have guidance. We have hope. We have a direct link to Spirit.

We have been put here as individuals,
for we are solely responsible
for the decisions that bring about
our own evolution.

Ultimately hope is the recognition of spirit guides and loving angels. Every person is connected with entities that help us each and every day. We need only ask for guidance. The more we recognize the existence of guides, the more open our connection to Spirit. Call it intuition or having a hunch—it is divine guidance.

> *During the Depression of the 1930s, Irene lost a brooch and had searched everywhere. She prayed to Saint Anthony, the patron saint of lost articles. Several days later when she was cooking in the kitchen, there was a knock on the back door. She saw a man standing there and assumed he would ask for food, but instead he asked for a pair of socks. She went to her room and took down the box where she kept mismatched socks. While looking for a warm pair she found her brooch. She returned to the kitchen with the socks only to find the man had gone.*
>
> *Irene knew the man at the kitchen door was Saint Anthony. Her prayers had been answered.*

Tapping into Hope

It seems daunting to be placed on this earth with little instruction and then be expected to live, love, and be happy. The guidelines we receive from society have often been misconstrued and manipulated in order to control man. We do not always sense the guidance and hope that are available to us.

Our spirit guides are a source of hope, enabling us to encounter adversity and learn life lessons. The Universal Truths of free will, karma, purity, love, truth, faith, and hope are defined in this book in human terms. Let them guide you on your true journey toward Spirit as you embrace unconditional love.

Affirmation of Hope

Today I choose to hold in my heart and mind an awareness of the guidance I give and receive. I believe this guidance will bring about the manifestation of all Universal Truths.

Prayer for Hope

Spirit, I open my higher consciousness to all the paths and obstacles Your universe sets forth. You provide hope, faith, and love to guide me. Thank You for all guidance, which I take to the world today. Thank you for the light of hope, my everlasting companion, illuminating my life's path in our darkest moments. Amen.

CHAPTER EIGHT

Life is not planned in a concrete manner. Our guides can look at our lives as if looking down at a chessboard. From above they can see the moves made and the individuals involved. We are a piece on the chessboard and can only see those directly around us. Our guides present us with every possible move, but we make the choice. Once that move is made, our guides reassess the board and then re-present the many choices at hand. The final result is to get to the end with the king intact. Learn your lessons and be a positive influence during this life. Life is not a game, but a spiritual journey of love and learning.

Connecting with Your Guide

Free will can seem daunting and intimidating. Fortunately our guides narrow our choices and help us achieve our highest path. No matter what choice we make along the way, we can still achieve our goal for this life. The path we take may be altered, but the lessons are still the same.

Spirit guides help clarify free will. They are our ultimate teachers here to help guide and comfort us. They help us see the many choices we have. Your freewill choice prevents psychics or clairvoyants from predicting the future, although they provide valid guidance. They can offer an alternate assessment of your situation through contact with spirit guides.

Incarnation on the earth plane is about learning lessons. These lessons bring us closer to Spirit. If needed, we are given more than one opportunity to learn the same lesson. If we listen, our guides will help us. Call it intuition or serendipity; our guides call our attention to opportunities each and every day. It is still our decision which choice we make and which path we take. Choose to be a positive influence on those lives you touch along the way.

Connecting with your guide is not difficult. When you feel as if you are arguing with yourself or talking to yourself, your guide is on the other side of that discussion. Inner guidance occurs while you are thinking or speaking. You may get on a roll or answer your own questions with an enlightened view. Listen! Evaluate the information. Start paying attention on these occasions. You are recognizing guidance, and you are accepting hope. A connection to your guide creates more confidence in your choices.

Your guide's voice comes from within. There is no right or wrong way to communicate with your guide. Do not worry if you do not have a name or an image by which to identify your guide. Listen and remain open. You were born with the gift of guidance and hope!

Some people worry that they are imagining the existence of guides. The key is to realize that when you see people in your mind or in your dreams, they are there. When they talk, they are talking to you. The more you listen, the more you hear. Intuitives merely listen more closely! Trust the first word or image entering your mind. Take a leap. Begin by acknowledging the role guidance has played in small successes. Allow your confidence in your guide to build. Don't budge from that confidence! Your guides will not lead you down the wrong path.

CHAPTER NINE

A crystal can assist you in your journey of seeking the Universal Truths. The crystals referred to in this book are clear quartz crystals. Quartz comes in many different forms: clear, smoky, rose, citrine, and amethyst, just to name a few. Quartz can form masses, clusters, or points.

Crystals are made up of subtle vibrations each attuned to a greater universal force. A crystal can work as a lightning rod. It is a transducer of energy. Crystals accept and adjust energy so that the holder can easily access it. This allows the energy we access from Spirit to be slowed down and our personal energy to be amplified. This role as an energy adjuster allows crystals to be an excellent tool in meditation.

Quartz crystals are piezoelectric. This means they have the ability to give off electrical impulses when their crystalline structure is compressed. This sets them apart from other crystalline structures and gives them exceptional value in the metaphysical world.

Thought is energy and energy is thought. Thoughts create. The energy (thoughts) stored inside these crystals can be tapped and transferred from the crystals to you. Quartz crystals with an isosceles triangle on one or more of their facets have information stored inside. These crystals are called teacher crystals. They contain information for the holder on the earth plane.

During meditation this information can be retrieved. To access this information, achieve a meditative state. Hold the crystal or place it on your third eye. The information relayed during this meditative state is from this crystal. This can be done on more than one occasion. By placing a crystal on your nightstand you can gather information during your sleep. You may notice triangles appearing or disappearing on certain crystals. They arise when there is information to be received. Once the information has been accessed, the triangle will disappear.

Preparing Your Crystal

Before using your crystals, they need to be cleansed of residual vibrations. This is done in a three-step process: absorbing residual energy, rinsing the residual energy away, and charging or re-energizing the crystal.

Step One

The first step is the absorption of any residual energy and negative energy. Cleansing is obtained by surrounding your crystal with sea salt to absorb unwanted energy. The crystal should remain in sea salt for twenty-four hours. Cleansing can also be obtained by immersing the crystal in the ocean. This process needs to be done for at least two minutes, longer if you feel it is necessary. A short prayer, such as the one below, should also be added when cleansing your crystals.

> *Spirit, please wash away the negativity contained in these crystals. Wash away the stagnant energy they hold. Allow these crystals to absorb the immense energy of the oceans charged daily with Your love. Allow these crystals to synchronize with Mother Earth. Please charge these crystals with Your love and allow them to transmit Your energy and knowledge into me and through me for eternity. Amen.*

Step Two

Step two is removing the crystal from the sea salt and rinsing it thoroughly with water. Water should be run over the crystal for seven minutes or placed in the rain for a few hours. Dissolving the sea salt with water moves the energy into this perfectly pure substance. Mother Earth can then reabsorb this energy into her mass, neutralizing and redistributing it appropriately. Dispose of leftover sea salt outside or in the garbage and let Mother Nature do the rest.

Step Three

Step three is charging. Place your crystal in direct sunlight from daybreak until dusk to charge or re-energize it. This can be done outside or through a window. After twenty-four hours your crystal is ready to use.

Charging Your Crystal

Crystals should first be charged with the white light of the sun in order to maximize their energy and connection with Spirit. They can then be charged with a certain color. Place your crystal on one of the solid color cards of the Crystal Charging Deck and expose it to sunlight from daybreak until dusk. The crystal is now charged with that color vibration. For example, when working on your base chakra, use a crystal charged with red. To do this, follow the directions below.

- Put a clear quartz crystal on a solid red card.
- Place it outside or on the windowsill where it will get the maximum sun exposure throughout the day.
- At the end of the day the crystal is charged with red.
- Use a signifier such as a sticker to remind you this quartz is charged with red, or keep the crystal on top of the red card when not in use.
- Place this crystal over your base chakra when doing Monday's meditation for free will (see Chapter 10).

Completely recharge all of your chakras by repeating these steps and charging other crystals with each of the colors corresponding to their chakras. Place the crystal on its corresponding chakra while lying flat on your back (see Chapter 10 for Meditations). Once you are done with the chakra meditation, say this simple prayer:

May the white light of God come into
my crown chakra and fully align, balance,
and energize all of my chakras.

Suggested Uses

You can charge your crystal with certain color vibrations in order to help you invoke the Universal Truth associated with that color. You can also charge crystals with specific thoughts. Below are additional ways to use your charged crystal.

- Place it on your windowsill or bedside table.

- Take a clear quartz crystal and place it over your third eye to charge it with the positive energy you will need to make the next big presentation. Visualize yourself making an impact on those who hear your message. Program your visualization into the crystal like a recorder. Carry that crystal with you, and it will help you remember what you need to say. Your presentation will be well received.

- Wrap it with copper wire and wear it as jewelry.

- Place it on your desk or table while working.

- In a quiet place, position the crystal on your forehead and ask for the wisdom it has to offer.

- Hold the crystal over your heart chakra and charge it with the green energy of loving relationships. Give that crystal to someone special and feel the energy. It is a precious gift for anyone, regardless of his or her belief system.

- Use your charged crystal in any respectful manner.

CHAPTER TEN

Many individuals feel they lack the discipline to meditate. The mind is like a puppy on a leash. It wants to tug, pull, tumble, and be free rather than be disciplined. Effective meditation is achieved through practice. Many people find it beneficial to record and play the instructions for themselves to assist in their sessions.

To achieve an effective meditative state:

- Find a quiet place.
- Sit in a comfortable chair with your feet flat on the floor and your spine straight, or lie flat on the floor with arms at your sides.
- Roll your head around from side to side, loosening your muscles.
- Close your eyes and concentrate on the intent of your meditation.
- Inhale deeply through your nose and exhale through your mouth.
- Take deep, slow cleansing breaths and allow each one to relax your body.
- While in this state, carry out the guided chakra meditations below. Converse with your spirit guide or guardian angel.

Chakra Meditation on Free Will

Meditation for Free Will: Place a clear quartz crystal charged with the color red on the base (root) chakra. This is located on top of the pelvic bone.

With the chakra meditation on free will we ground ourselves to the physical in order to learn and understand our lessons on earth. This meditation opens your earthly intentions for guidance from a higher source. This guidance will help clarify the opportunities and choices as you enact the Universal Truth of free will.

Free will vibrates with the color red and with the base chakra. The base chakra is at the base (root) of the spine and at the pubic bone.

- To begin this meditation, place a clear quartz crystal that has been charged with the color red on your base chakra. (For instructions on charging your crystal, see Chapter 9).

- Breathe deeply.

- Imagine the root chakra vibrating and encompassed by a beautiful warm red. This color spins clockwise, around and around, warming the entire area and energizing your physical body.

- In the midst of this spinning, envision the bright white light of Spirit pouring down, infusing your crown, your third eye, your throat, your heart, your solar plexus, your sacral plexus, and finally, connecting to the spinning ball of red energy at your root chakra.

- You have made the divine connection between Spirit and your earthly choices. Hold this energy and feel it move within you.

- When you feel ready, close your crown chakra by envisioning the white light being disconnected from the source. Imagine your crown as a shutter of a camera and close that shutter. Continue closing each chakra. Close your root chakra where the red light is disconnected from its source. It will continue to glow within you. Count slowly to five and imagine yourself rising to consciousness.

- Breathe freely and acknowledge the lessons of choice!

Chakra Meditation on Karma

Meditation for Karma: Place a clear quartz crystal charged with the color orange on the sacral plexus chakra. This is located just below the navel.

This meditation refers to all of the lower chakras in the body. Review the diagram on page 12, which shows the locations of the chakras, before reading further and carrying out the meditation.

With the chakra meditation on karma we invoke our creative energy. This meditation opens your awareness to the lessons you are teaching and learning through your actions, reactions, and interactions.

Karma vibrates with the color orange and with the sacral chakra. This is the meeting ground between the physical (root chakra: red) and the intellectual (solar plexus chakra: yellow). In order to learn and understand our lessons on earth, we bring together these qualities of the physical and the intellectual.

- To begin this meditation, place a clear quartz crystal that has been charged with the color orange on your sacral chakra.

- Breathe deeply, pulling in the crisp, clear white light of Spirit through your crown chakra. As this tunnel of light passes through each chakra, imagine the root chakra vibrating a beautiful warm red. It spins around and around clockwise at your base, warming the entire area and energizing your physical body. As this continues, imagine the bright yellow spin of your solar plexus. Spinning and energizing, the two energies grow and meet with vitality at your sacrum, energizing the lower area of your body and generating an orange glow.

- You have now made the divine connection between Spirit and your karmic lessons. What images come before you? Is there someone you resent or someone who makes you angry? Is there someone to whom you are grateful or someone you respect? Take your time and let him or her appear.

- Send out energy of gratitude for the opportunities this soul has offered you. If that soul resisted change or altered your path through actions benign or malign, send thanks for being put on a path of goodness.

- Let others come. Rather than regarding them in terms of what they did to you or how they made you feel, simply send them gratitude for joining you on the path you chose together. Send love, gratitude, and forgiveness. Embrace the lesson. Hold this energy in the orange light at your sacrum and feel it move within you as you breathe.

- When you feel ready, close your crown chakra by envisioning the white light being disconnected from the source. Imagine your crown as a shutter of a camera and close that shutter. Continue closing each chakra. Close your sacrum where the orange light is disconnected from its source. It will continue to glow within you. Count slowly to five and imagine yourself rising to consciousness.

- Breathe freely and rejoice in your actions.

Chakra Meditation on Purity

Meditation for Purity: Place a clear quartz crystal charged with the color yellow on the solar plexus chakra. This is located over your stomach.

This meditation refers to two of the chakras in the body. It is useful to review the diagram on page 12, which shows the locations of the chakras, before reading further and carrying out this meditation.

With the chakra meditation on purity we invoke our positive thoughts and our optimism. Purity vibrates with the color yellow and with the solar plexus, which governs the stomach area, skin, nervous system, and senses. In order to purify the body, begin with the thoughts and attitudes you embrace each day. This meditation reformulates the beliefs that have limited you and replaces them with limitless aspirations.

- To begin this meditation, place a clear quartz crystal that has been charged with the color yellow on your solar plexus, the center chakra in your stomach region.
- Breathe deeply.
- Surround yourself with the white, protective divine light of Spirit and ask the purification process to begin.
- The crystal is an open window to the love and purity of divine Spirit. Concentrate on the quartz as it cleanses and fills you with the purity of intellectual yellow.
- Breathe deeply and pull in the crisp, clear white light of Spirit. As this tunnel of light passes through each chakra,

yellow begins to fill your toes, your feet, your legs, and spreads up through your torso.

- Soon the purification process encompasses your entire body. Your body is fully saturated with this pure yellow light, which is assimilated into your body's molecules. The crystalline structures within your body are recharged.

- Your crown chakra now radiates the pure glow of yellow.

- Imagine the yellow light becoming more saturated with crystalline specks. As your entire body continues to be purified, the yellow light is transformed into a crystalline pure white light.

- After the meditation close your solar plexus as a shutter in a camera closes. Then close your crown chakra in the same way.

- You emerge from this meditation feeling refreshed with all feelings of negativity and confusion dissolved.

- Breathe freely and allow your thoughts to create!

Chakra Meditation for Love

Meditation for Love: Place a clear quartz crystal charged with the color green on the heart chakra. This is located between your breasts on your chest area.

This meditation refers to all the chakras in the body. It is useful to review the diagram on page 12, which shows the locations of the chakras, before reading further and carrying out the meditation.

With this chakra meditation we invoke love in our relationships with others and ourselves. This meditation opens your awareness to your relationship with the world around you. While meditating, reflect on your relationship to self and how this influences your relationships with everyone and everything in the universe. Before beginning this meditation spend a few moments breathing deeply and saying softly as you exhale, "I love myself."

- Place a clear quartz crystal charged with the color green on your heart chakra. Imagine the heart chakra vibrating a beautiful emerald green. It spins around and around clockwise at your heart, radiating and refreshing your entire physical body.

- As you breathe deeply, imagine you are filling each part of your body with the pure light of green. Envision green of the healthiest, richest grass you have ever seen.

- Breathe in.

- Fill your toes, your feet, your shins, and moving upward, your entire body with the pure green light of love.

- As you breathe, let the green light flow through your body. Feel each molecule in your body vibrating in harmony to the green light of love. When you are ready, release the green light through your toes and your fingertips. It flows out to the world in streams and can be focused on somebody or something.

- When you feel ready, close your crown chakra by envisioning the white light being disconnected from the source. Imagine your crown as a shutter of a camera and close that shutter. Continue closing each chakra down to your root chakra. Disconnect the green light of the heart chakra from its source. It will continue to glow within you. Count slowly to five and imagine yourself rising to consciousness.

- You emerge from this meditation feeling refreshed with all feelings of negativity resolved.

• Breathe freely and hold love in your heart.

Chakra Meditation for Truth

Meditation for Truth: Place a clear quartz crystal charged with the color blue on the throat chakra. This is located at your throat region.

This meditation refers to many of the chakras in the body. It is useful to review the diagram on page 12, which shows the locations of the chakras, before reading further and carrying out the meditation.

• Before you begin this meditation, place a clear quartz crystal charged with the color blue on your throat chakra.

• Breathe deeply.

• Slowly pull down the white light of Spirit through your crown chakra. As this beautiful, sparkling white light touches each and every aspect of your being, you are enlightened by the power of Spirit's Universal Truths.

• Draw light from your third eye, the chakra of faith. Draw in all of the divine energy from each of your chakra centers to focus on your throat area. As Spirit, faith, and truth converge around your throat, you become more empowered to speak the truth as Spirit defines it. Your throat chakra becomes charged with truth.

• Your truth is enhanced by the purest thoughts.

- When you feel ready, close your crown chakra by envisioning the white light being disconnected from the source. Imagine your crown as a shutter of a camera and close that shutter. Continue closing each chakra down to your root chakra. Your throat energy center continues to glow with the blue light of truth. Count slowly to five and imagine yourself rising to consciousness.

- You emerge from this meditation feeling refreshed with all feelings of negativity resolved. Speak and act according to the best intentions in both your freewill choices and your karmic relationships throughout the day.

- Breathe freely and live with the best of intentions.

Chakra Meditation for Faith

Meditation for Faith: Place a clear quartz crystal charged with the color indigo on your third eye. This is located on your forehead between your eyes.

With the chakra meditation on faith we invoke our spirit guides. Faith is generated in the third eye chakra, which vibrates in accordance with the color indigo. The third eye chakra can be looked at as a window. Through this window we can see our path—a path we can undertake with confidence by maintaining faith.

This meditation refers to many of the chakras in the body. It is useful to review the diagram on page 12, which shows the locations of the chakras, before reading further and carrying out this meditation.

- To begin this meditation, place a clear quartz crystal charged with the color indigo on your third eye chakra.

- Breathe deeply.

- Surround yourself with the white, protective divine light of Spirit and ask the purification process to begin.

- Concentrate upon the quartz crystal and believe it is bathing you in the comforting faith of indigo. Channel indigo down through your crown chakra and into your shoulders, torso, hips, legs, feet, and toes. The comforting and secure blanket of indigo covers your entire body.

- Using your imagination and your third eye, envision three doors.

- Cloak yourself in the color of indigo and walk up to a door. There is not an incorrect door.

- Open the door. You see your spirit guide. Exchange greetings and embrace this loving entity. Have a conversation. Ask questions and take time to listen. Do not feel it is your imagination, for it is your spirit guide offering hope. Allow the conversation to continue and go with the moment.

- With your spirit guide still present, imagine your body is fully saturated with the color indigo. This saturation fully recharges the crystalline structures in your body.

- Ask your spirit guide to help you arrange the energy field around your third eye chakra so that you can better respond to cues which will reveal your path. As opposed to the other meditations, close your third eye chakra first, as a shutter in a camera closes.

- When you feel ready, close your crown chakra by envisioning the white light being disconnected from the source. Imagine your crown as a shutter of a camera and close that shutter. Continue closing each chakra down to your root chakra. Your third eye continues to glow within you. Count slowly to five and imagine yourself rising to consciousness.

- You emerge from this meditation empowered with the foundation on which you will build your beliefs.
- Breathe freely and walk with faith.

Chakra Meditation for Hope

Meditation for Hope (Step One): Place a clear quartz crystal charged with the white color of hope on your third eye chakra center. This is located on your forehead between your eyes.

Meditation for Hope (Step Two): Move the clear quartz crystal charged with the white color of hope to your crown chakra center. This is located at the top of your head.

This meditation refers to multiple chakras in the body. It is useful to review the diagram on page 12, which shows the locations of the chakras, before reading further and carrying out the meditation.

- To begin this meditation, place a clear quartz crystal charged with the white light of the sun on the third eye chakra.

- Breathe deeply. As you breathe, open your third eye.

- With each breath, starting at your toes, slowly relax each muscle in your body.

- Fill your entire body with the white light of hope. Ask your body to process all the divine white light. As you are filled with this white light, ask to recognize hope in every aspect of your life.

- As you continue to be filled with the white light, feel your third eye closing as the shutter of a camera closes.

- Move the crystal from your third eye to your crown chakra. Feel the crown chakra opening.

- With the crown chakra open, send forth the white light of hope. You are a prism. You are hope. You have passed through the great door and have become a walking light of hope to the world. Rejoice, for all things are possible!

- When you feel ready, close your crown chakra by envisioning the white light being disconnected from the source. Imagine your crown as a shutter of a camera and close that shutter. Continue closing each chakra, down to your root chakra. Your crown center will continue to glow within you. Count slowly to five and imagine yourself rising to consciousness.

- You emerge from this meditation containing the hope of the world.

- Breathe freely and walk in the light.

CONCLUSION

We have introduced seven Universal Truths. These truths are the foundation for many theological rules provided throughout time. These seven Universal Truths are linked to a day, a color, a number, a tone, an affirmation, a prayer, and a chakra meditation. You can practice each truth on the given day, but do not hesitate to recognize all truths every day.

You will become adept at realizing you are here to teach and to learn. The situation in front of you is something you can learn from and an opportunity for growth. You will see fewer injustices and more lessons. You will see fewer obstacles and more opportunities for personal growth. You will change your outlook. You will become a better person, a better parent, a better employer, and a better employee. *You will become a better spiritual being.*

You will teach others through your practice. It will become second nature to you. By simply realizing everything is a lesson to be taught and learned, life will become fun again.

Sometimes in order to get to those peaks we must "walk through the valley." There will be heartache and heartbreak. There will be situations seemingly insurmountable. That is life. Not everything is a joy, and not everything is wondrous. There are times when we will be carrying others through the valley. Always remember, these are lessons to be learned and taught. Things DO happen for a reason, and situations ALWAYS work out for the best.

The next time you have a difficult interaction, ask yourself these two questions: "What can be learned?" and "What can be taught?" Search your heart. Should you become involved or not participate? Remind yourself of free will. Think of the choices driving this situation. Keep purity in your heart and always strive to do the right thing. Be true to yourself and the world. *Remember, you are never alone, and help is only a thought away.* This will allow you to be a better person. This will help you understand unconditional love. This will elevate you as a person and a spirit of divine light.

Thank Spirit each and every day for giving us this wonderful world. Let us all pray in our own way so that we may understand each other. We are all working toward the same goal. We embrace more similarities than differences. Realize that no matter what name we assign to our Divine Creator, this wondrous entity is the same for all!

May this book and the information it holds bring love, peace, and abundance for all who read it.

We bid you a joyous and pleasant life path.

The Bristol Clinic opened its doors in January 2005. It provides insight to individuals attempting to grasp what their disease is about and why/how they specifically have been affected. Healing is generated from within and begins with an understanding that responsibility for one's dis-ease is not about blame or shame; it is about the ability to respond. Integrated Health Concepts helps individuals understand their current health challenges so that they can respond in a positive and healing manner.

It is our desire to help those who seek a higher answer to their well-being. In order to deliver cutting-edge health care we assembled the best delivery team possible. The combination of an intuitive healer and a physician enables us to facilitate understanding of why the dis-ease manifests. Through understanding the root of the problem ANY dis-ease can be treated as a personal gift of insight.

We are interested in your needs. Please contact us with any questions, concerns, or comments.

James H. Schrenker, M.D.
Catherine S. Poole, M.F.A.

For more information or to request a client application form, log on to www.BristolClinic.com, call our office at 423-968-9669, or e-mail us at info@integratedconcepts.org

integrated concepts publishing

Sapling Grove Professional Building
240 Medical Park Boulevard, Suite 1000
Bristol, Tennessee 37620
Tel.877.405.7200 Email: order@everydaylessons.com

Address

NAME _____ COMPANY _____

ADDRESS _____

CITY _____ STATE _____ ZIP _____

TELEPHONE NUMBER _____ EMAIL ADDRESS _____

Description	Quantity		Amount
Everyday Lessons: Understanding the Events, Interactions, and Attitudes That Make Up Your Life (Hardback) ISBN: 0-9759245-2-4	_____	x $24.95	$ _____
		+ $4.95 S/H (per book)	$ _____
		Total	$ _____
Everyday Lessons: Understanding the Events, Interactions, and Attitudes That Make Up Your Life (Paperback) ISBN: 0-9759245-7-5	_____	x $15.95	$ _____
		+ $4.95 S/H (per book)	$ _____
		Total	$ _____
Pocket Pack (Affirmation Card and Universal Key Card combo)	_____	x $12.50	$ _____
		+ $4.95 S/H (per pack)	$ _____
		Total	$ _____
Affirmation Card Pack	_____	x $6.95	$ _____
		+ $4.95 S/H (per pack)	$ _____
		Total	$ _____
Universal Key Card Pack	_____	x $5.95	$ _____
		+ $4.95 S/H (per pack)	$ _____
		Total	$ _____
Crystal Charging Kit (includes seven color cards and seven clear quartz crystals)	_____	x $34.95	$ _____
		+ $8.95 S/H (per kit)	$ _____
		Total	$ _____

I wish to pay by

○ CASH
○ CHECK
○ MONEY ORDER

○ VISA   ○ MASTERCARD

CARD NUMBER
☐☐☐☐☐☐☐☐☐☐☐☐☐☐☐☐☐☐

EXPIRATION DATE (REQUIRED)
MONTH   YEAR
☐☐ / ☐☐

_____
CARDHOLDER'S NAME

Checks and/or money orders
are to be made payable to:
Integrated Concepts Publishing

SUB-TOTAL	$ _____
SALES TAX (Indiana Residents add 6% state sales tax)	$ _____
GRAND TOTAL	$ _____

_____
SIGNATURE

This edition designed by:

Tangent Design Group, Inc.
Chicago

(TEL) 773.394.8430 (WEB) www.tangentinc.com

Cover illustration courtesy of:

Anthony Droege
Title: Fall Splendor ©2000
Oil 69" x 89"

Professor Droege is the Chairman of the
Fine Arts Department at Indiana University
South Bend, South Bend, Indiana.

For more information about purchasing
Professor Droege's work or to schedule
a commission, contact him through our
website www.everydaylessons.com.